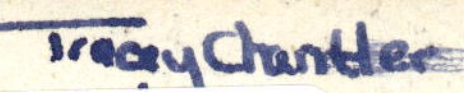

Health care together

Training Exercises for Health Workers in Community Based Programmes
Edited by Mary P. Johnston and Susan B. Rifkin

Tracey Chantler PhD MSc MCH Adv Dip Ed & Dev RGN
Research Fellow in Health Services and Systems Research & James Martin Fellow
George Centre for Healthcare Innovation, University of Oxford
Richard Doll Building, Old Road Campus
Roosevelt Drive, Oxford, OX3 7LF, United Kingdom
Tel: +44(0)1865 617207 Skype: tchantler1
Email: tracey.chantler@georgecentre.ox.ac.uk www.georgecentre.ox.ac.uk

First published 1987
Reprinted 1991, 1993, 1994

Published by THE MACMILLAN PRESS LTD
London and Basingstoke
Associated companies and representatives in Accra, Auckland, Delhi, Dublin, Gaborone, Hamburg, Harare, Hong Kong, Kuala Lumpur, Lagos, Manzini, Melbourne, Mexico City, Nairobi, New York, Singapore, Tokyo

ISBN 0–333–44348–9

Printed in Hong Kong

A catalogue record for this book is available from the British Library.

Published in conjunction with Teaching Aids at Low Cost, PO Box 49, St Albans, Hertfordshire, AL1 4AX.

TALC received assistance in the production of this book as a low cost edition from the Swedish International Development Authority.

The authors and publishers wish to thank TALC for the use of illustrations on pages 2, 8, 32, 54, 65 and 76.

Contents

Foreword

Primary Health Care has the potential to make a much bigger impact on the health of the people of the world than any other health development. Yet this potential can only be achieved if health workers accept approaches to their work which are markedly different from the conventional paradigms of western medicine. Foremost amongst these new approaches is the need to base health care within communities and to work *with* communities in sharing knowledge and skills, in jointly deciding on plans for health care and in generally seeking to develop and strengthen the communities' capacity to care for itself.

It is sometimes thought that a community based approach is the natural way of working for all health workers. Yet experience shows that conventional medical training tends to lead to a directive style of leadership, a rather rigid approach to solving 'their' problems and great difficulties in listening to and responding to the feelings and ideas expressed in a community. The community based approach is not the normal outcome of conventional training and therefore new approaches to the training of health workers must be explored. These will focus on the development of appropriate attitudes and the strengthening of skills (especially in the area of communication) that have only rarely been explicitly taught to health personnel.

Unfortunately, teachers who are persuaded of the value of the philosophy outlined above usually receive little help in their teaching. They may wish to teach the communication skills and the community oriented attitudes, but they have little experience of being taught these things themselves and few teachers' manuals give detailed and specific guidance.

Therefore *Health Care Together* is a very welcome contribution. It provides a wealth of tried and tested learning exercises which teachers may use to help their students learn different attitudes and new skills. The exercises are provided in sufficiently detailed form, so that teachers can use them immediately. However, the book is not prescriptive and teachers are encouraged to adapt the exercises to suit local requirements.

It might be thought that such exercises were only of relevance to those health workers with the lowest level of education. However, I believe that training of all levels of health care personnel could be strengthened by incorporating learning exercises of the type described here. Where these exercises are used the students will be better able to respond flexibly to the needs of communities, to listen to what the people are saying and to help them find solutions to their problems. In this way, *Health Care Together* will contribute to the effectiveness of Primary Health Care as a strategy for achieving improved health throughout the world.

Fred Abbatt
Department of International Community Health,
Liverpool School of Tropical Medicine.

Introduction

In 1978 over 150 governments, members of the World Health Organisation (WHO), became signatories to the Alma Ata Declaration to support Primary Health Care (PHC) as national policy. In doing so, they pledged to pursue the development of a health care system which shifted priorities from curative, institution based, professionally dominated care, to a new approach. This approach stressed preventive, community based care designed to meet the needs of the majority of the world's people living in poverty. In retrospect, these noble intentions have been difficult to realise. There are many reasons for this. In addition to political and social problems, a major reason has also been the lack of training and experience of health care providers in community work.

In the past, health services have been structured in a way that gave providers limited action with community groups. What interaction developed focused mainly on the provision of mobile health services, outreach clinics, vertically structured mass preventive programmes, such as immunisation campaigns or mosquito spraying programmes, and sporadic health education talks. These activities encouraged health personnel to limit their community concerns to delivering a specific intervention. They did not encourage health providers to develop a broad, sustaining relationship with the community members. As a result, members of the community often thought that health services were oriented to the providers rather than intended beneficiaries.

The formulation of the concept of PHC recognised the shortcomings of the existing health care system. In seeking to radically and rapidly improve the health of those who were increasingly denied access to care because it was inaccessible, unaffordable and unacceptable, PHC put community participation to the fore as the means by which to gain health improvements. It called for those involved to re-orient their tasks to extend beyond mere provision of services to building up, supporting and maintaining the involvement of each community in its own care.

The community based orientation of PHC has demanded that health providers seek ways of gaining the skills necessary to promote community involvement. Few training programmes, particularly those based in medical schools, have found ways and means of meeting the increasing call for people to promote and implement community based health programmes. There is a growing demand that this need be met.

To date there are at least two books that have begun to address this need. They are *Teaching Health Workers* by Fred Abbatt and Rosemary McMahon[1] and *Helping Health Workers Learn* by David Werner and Bill

1 Fred Abbatt and Rosemary McMahon, *Teaching Health Care Workers*, London: Macmillan, 1985 and David Werner and Bill Bower, *Helping Health Workers Learn*, USA: Hesperian Foundation, 1982. Both these books are available from Teaching Aids at Low Cost (TALC), PO Box 49, St. Albans, Herts, AL1 4AX, U.K.

Bower[1]. This book is an additional contribution to this literature. Its purpose is to provide a series of exercises to support the type of learning that is suggested by Abbatt, McMahon, Werner and Bower. In other words, it is to help health workers develop skills in group formation, communication, discussion, team building, leadership and community development planning that will assist them in creating and sustaining community efforts in both individual and community health improvements.

This book is designed to be used by those who train community based health workers. It is a book for trainers. However, many of the exercises need not be confined to the classroom. They may be used by health workers in their own communities to build and support community action for health care. The exercises in this book have, for the most part, been compiled by a team of trainers at Yayasan Indonesia Sejatera (YIS) and have been used extensively in Indonesia. However, they have also been widely used in training undertaken by the Asian Community Health Action Network (ACHAN), with groups throughout Asia which have been associated with ACHAN and in schools of medicine and public health in England and other parts of the developed world. They have been developed and used, in many cases, by people who work in adult education. Credit to their work has been given where appropriate.

These exercises have been used successfully in a wide range of cultures, in both developed and developing societies, to begin to develop skills for community work among heterogenous groups of people from medical doctors to semi-literate rural community health workers. They, therefore, have proved not to be bound by culture or education. In addition, while this book addresses the problems of health workers, these skills are not limited to this profession. They are skills necessary for anyone who works among groups of people in supporting these groups to improve their lives.

The first chapter of this book reviews the failures of the health care system that led to Alma Ata and describes the emerging alternative by focusing on the needs of community health care and the implications of the health care profession. Chapter 2 is a case study of how PHC based on community participation and development grew in one country, Indonesia, and how some of the training demands of this new emphasis were met. Chapter 3 highlights some of the principles of teaching and education on which the exercises we present are based. Chapters 4 through 9 include 41 exercises divided into the groups of skills which they seek to develop. These include: group formation skills, communication skills, team work skills, leadership skills, and community development skills.

This book is a result of both authors' involvement of over 10 years in training programmes in Asia. It has grown out of a repeated demand by numerous trainees to have in written form exercises in which they have participated. We have compiled these exercises in answer to this request. We owe a great deal of thanks to both YIS and ACHAN whose commitment to both community based health programmes and participatory training programmes has greatly enlarged our understanding of health problems in developing societies and the need to support all efforts at widening community participation in health care.

Many people have been critical in helping us to finally get these exercises into print. We would like to thank particularly our colleagues in YIS and ACHAN and Professor David Morley who constantly urged us to put together this publication. We also wish to thank Pat Harman and John MacDonald who read the manuscript and offered invaluable suggestions. We would also like to thank Owi from Indonesia for adding life to *Health Care Together* with his imaginative illustrations. And a big thanks to Madeleine Green who did the typing.

Mary P. Johnston
Solo, Indonesia.

Susan B. Rifkin
London, England.

1 *What kind of health care?*

Primary Health Care (PHC) has called for a new approach to health care. Rather than focusing on doctors curing people in hospitals, it emphasises improved health which is community based and is rooted in individual and community efforts. There are several reasons for this new approach. By reviewing the most important, we can see why this approach developed and what implications it has for the training of future health professionals.

In the period which followed the Second World War and the rapid 'decolonialisation' of many countries in what came to be called the 'third world', there began a questioning about the way in which health care services had been delivered. The newly independent countries often were left with the vestiges of an old system which was very expensive to maintain and was virtually devoid of a preventive infrastructure which had improved health patterns in the industrial countries a half century earlier. In addition, studies began to show that health was not merely a problem of disease. Rather it was, for the majority of the world's population, a problem of the cycle of poverty, malnutrition, and chronic illness.

These new views about health improvements put into focus the problem of resources. Again, studies showed that health expenditure, often regarded as a 'bottomless pit', was absorbed by large curative institutions and new medical technologies with the result that those who most needed the services had neither the money nor opportunity to gain access to care. Other studies suggested that scarce health resources would be better spent on developing good preventive measures so that the cured would not return to the same environment to catch the same disease.

Finally, there was a growing view among both medical professionals and health planners that the rapid and radical health improvements which everyone sought were not to be found in new developments in medical science and technology. These improvements would be realised in what individuals did to and for themselves. Individual and community choices about health care strongly supported by the medical professional's knowledge and resources were the key to health improvements and the basis on which PHC was formulated.

PHC was proposed and adopted by the member states of the World Health Organisation in Alma Ata in 1978. PHC highlighted the need to provide health care which was accessible, acceptable and appropriate to the health problems of all people. This came to mean placing emphasis on preventive rather than curative care, on health centre rather than hospital treatment and on the use of paramedics rather than medical professionals for doing routine tasks. It also came to mean viewing health as a part of total human development rather than a function of advances in medical science and technology and community participation as critical in decisions about and involvement in the activities for health care improvements.

PHC did not mean cosmetic surgery for the existing health care delivery system. It meant a total re-orientation of that system to address health not as a disease problem but a problem of poverty, of social justice and equity and most important, of people who had different problems and concerns. PHC was not to be a replicated formula to solve the world's health problems but a new approach responsive to individuals and communities with their own needs, resources and potentials.

One implication of the PHC approach was the necessity for a larger role for the individual/community in health care and for a less dominant role for the professional. However, the traditional training of health professionals has not provided a framework which allows this shift to be made easily. Health workers have been taught using lecture methods which assume that the person is an empty vessel and the teacher is present to fill the vessel up. While this method is useful for memorising anatomical facts and diagnosing diseases, it does not provide health professionals with skills necessary to interact effectively with those who

seek the application of their memorised knowledge. This lack of skill not only exists in the closed health worker/patient relationship, it also exists on a much larger scale when health workers attempt to carry out their tasks with larger community groups. This failure often compromises the credibility of the health worker making the very valuable service he or she has to offer unacceptable to those who need it most.

The emphasis of PHC on community involvement has revealed a critical need to find an alternative teaching approach in order that skills which promote positive human relationships can be developed by health workers. These skills, unlike the knowledge of medical science and technology, cannot be memorised. Rather they are gained and perfected by having health workers seek their own solutions to the problems of interaction they confront. In other words, they do not appear in textbook form with a stated problem and a stated answer. Instead, health workers must learn and gain confidence about how to handle situations which differ each time they appear. They must develop a flexible approach to problems and must not panic if the approach they chose does not work in any one situation. They must be prepared to try to find another solution.

Teaching these skills, obviously, does not come through lectures. It comes through participation and experience. For those used to a rigid educational form, it means acquiring a new set of attitudes and ideas about teaching and learning. It means taking a view that learning is a process that is continuous and is not ended when the class is dismissed or the accreditation given. It also means the concepts of 'listening to others', 'having a dialogue' and 'learning from others' become critical to developing these skills.

For health professionals acquiring an attitude based on exchange rather than preaching is not easy. Most often, they have little experience to suggest that imparting knowledge does not necessarily mean that this knowledge is acted upon by those who receive it. In addition, skills needed to promote this approach do not produce immediate results. Unlike a pill to relieve pain which produces quickly the desired effect, group interaction needs careful nurturing and grows over a long period of time.

The success of PHC, in part, will depend on how successful health workers are in gaining confidence and participation of community people in working for health improvements. Gaining skills which will help workers motivate and gain commitment of lay people to become involved in their own health care is critical. While it may seem this call is both difficult and idealistic, it does not need to be. The following chapter describes how the re-orientation was undertaken in one programme expanded to a national scale. The rest of this volume discusses and presents a series of exercises that can be used to begin to develop community interaction and support skills. PHC emphasises the human factor. In this book are some ideas about how the factor can be understood and supported by health workers to enable health improvements to become a reality particularly to those who need it most.

2 *Together with whom? An Indonesian story*

A decade before the Declaration of Alma Ata a small team of doctors, paramedics, social workers and an agriculturalist began their search for a more appropriate health delivery system. Why, they asked, did children, cured of malnutrition at the local clinic, present in exactly the same condition a year later? Why did tuberculosis patients fail to improve? Why did children die of diarrhoea? Why? why? and more whys!

Banjarnegara, a poor Regency in Central Java, Indonesia, was one of the first areas where this group began tentative experiments in their attempt to find an answer to these questions or, even better still, a way out. Their efforts led to organising volunteer health workers, weighing programmes for children under five, environmental health measures, and even agricultural activities. The local communities were actively involved in all. A community health programme was taking shape.

At first activities were organised through a private rural clinic. However, as the programme grew, increasing interest was shown by doctors, universities and others from beyond Banjarnegara. From within, too, developments were being followed closely by the Regency doctor and the head of the Regency (*bupati*), both men of vision. The day arrived when the head of the Regency suggested that the government health service consider adopting and spreading this approach to other villages throughout the Regency. But the head of the Regency and the doctor faced a daunting task. How could they expand a programme covering five or six villages to eventually cover a Regency of 279 villages? To further complicate the situation several government departments would need to be involved in the multi-faceted programme. They decided that the initial investment should be for the development of human resources. The first step must be to prepare the manpower necessary to implement the programme with its radically different approach. Policy makers, managers and field workers would need to change their orientation from curative, institutional health care to an approach with its emphasis on the promotion of healthy living.

Thus a massive training programme was begun which, one and a half decades later, still continues. The training programme commenced with a cross sectoral workshop on community health management involving Regency government department heads, followed by a course for health workers. Through their attempts to initiate community activities these workers became acutely aware that the support of community leaders was essential. In response to this need a series of courses for formal and informal village leaders were held. These leaders in turn pointed out that they could do little without the support of both the community and their immediate superiors, the district heads. Hence the training programme in Banjarnegara grew in response to the needs of the programme, and to this day training continues to play a meaningful role in sustaining the continual expansion and maintenance of the primary health care programme in Banjarnegara.

Let us examine this training programme more closely. The trainers charged with designing the original training activities were in a quandary. The trainees were adults with widely varying formal education backgrounds - from illiterates to university graduates. Their experience was extensive and they knew the local situation far more intimately than any of the trainers. However, the heterogenous backgrounds of the participants was not the only challenge. The trainees had to acquire specific attitudes and skills to prepare them for action. Take, for example, the health workers who participated in the first training. They had to be imbued with enthusiasm for an approach to health care advocating active community participation, and acquire some of the basic skills needed for its implementation. How could the training effectively reinforce an approach which placed primary responsibility for healthy living on the people, rather than on the health service?

The key had to be participation. Throughout the training the trainers would need to provide repeated examples, or models, of how the health worker should function in a primary health care programme. The trainees would be most effectively convinced of the relevancy and potential of primary health care if they gained direct experience with this approach during the training. If, for example, the health worker must begin to respect the community's ability to participate in planning activities, the trainer would need to involve the trainees in planning the course. The trainees should not only hear about participation, but experience it. They should not only talk about cooperation but endeavour to cooperate with other trainees.

A series of lectures would obviously set the wrong example. Past experience indicated that adults who are treated like empty barrels to be filled with knowledge, usually end up in confusion, often expressed through headaches, a common symptom of mental constipation! And worse still, they gain no clear idea of what they must do after the training. To repeat such an approach would be irrelevant in the Banjarnegara situation where the major goal of the training programme was to produce *action*.

Therefore, given this background, the trainers decided to design a curriculum based on the probable tasks of a community health worker. A list of tasks was made based on interviews with the workers, plus the trainers past experience with community health activities. Knowledge, skills and attitudes required to carry out each task were then worked out. From this it was not too difficult to decide on course content, resulting in a tentative curriculum. On the first day of the training the health workers were asked to express what they hoped to gain from the course. These hopes were then combined with the tentative curriculum and a timetable drawn up together.

During this training, and all subsequent courses, the trainers endeavoured to involve the trainees as actively as possible, through discussion groups, tackling local problems, case studies, games and role plays. In this way the trainees became absorbed in the process of self-development and the acquisition of skills, and obtained deeper understanding of the community and its health problems. A brief assessment each day enabled the trainees and trainers to check out the relevancy of the day's contents and to set the direction for the following day. The training culminated with each participant writing a Plan of Action outlining what she or he planned to do immediately after the conclusion of the course. These plans of action proved to be a useful indicator of each participant's mastery of the course and commitment upon completion of the course. The plans of action also provided a 'handle' for follow up supervision of the health workers' activities in the community.

Although later training courses were refined and content adjusted to the needs of each group, the basic sequence of training activities remained the same:

- group formation exercises (e.g. Introductions, Drawing Up Expectations);
- attitude formation exercises (e.g. Distortions in Communication, Rumour Clinic, Drawing Together, The Dynamic Discussion);
- skill development and attitude reinforcement (e.g. Guess What is Needed, Consolidation of Social Preparation, Making the Longest Line and a Field Visit);
- plan of action.

Participatory methodology has now been used by the trainers in the Banjarnegara programme for more than 15 years. We have used the methodology in a multitude of situations, ranging from two day to two month courses for volunteer health workers, field workers, middle level managers, policy makers and others throughout Indonesia and beyond. For us the participatory approach in training has proved highly appropriate and effective for developing attitudes, deepening motivation and improving skills. After all these years we have no hesitation in recommending participatory training as an excellent tool for attaining human development.

3 A guide to using training exercises

There are few adult learners, and even fewer trainers, who have not been exposed, to some extent, to formal education. Most of us can clearly recall sitting in rows in a class with a teacher before us talking at us: the source of wisdom imparting fragments of that wisdom to the ignorant. Whether this was only a brief experience, or one of one and a half to two decades, it was probably highly impressionable. One proof of this can be seen from the behaviour of people in adult training situations. There is a strong tendency for them to take on the role of the teacher of their childhood, or the pupil of their memory. The trainer repeats the behaviour of the respected and honoured teacher filling her or his pupils' heads with knowledge, whereas the trainee assumes the passive role of the pupil absorbing the teacher's wisdom.

For several decades educators have been questioning the efficacy of this approach and their long quest for alternatives has resulted in significant changes in approaches to adult education, and even in

Seminar pulling in knowledge

the world of formal education. They have attempted to adjust to life situations and there are some who even speak of emancipation and liberation through learning experiences. These developments, along with our own experience, have had a powerful influence on the form of our adult training activities.

An adult's perception of the world differs markedly from that of a child. Knowles, a well known thinker in non formal education, has pinpointed four basic factors differentiating adults from children:

1 an adult prefers to be independent;
2 an adult has extensive experience;
3 an adult recognises the need to learn and is willing to learn;
4 an adult is predominantly oriented to the present.

These four factors alone have immense implications concerning the ways in which adults learn effectively. Take methodology as an example. If we reflect on our own preferred learning style and the preferences of several friends, we will find that each adult has his or her own particular style of learning. Some may learn best through reading, or by experimenting, whereas others may have a strong preference for discussing a subject with an expert, participating in a problem solving session with colleagues, or listening to a lecture. This simple exercise illustrates that adults (and probably children too if schools take the trouble to investigate) have learning styles which differ from one another and vary from one situation to another. For the trainer this has great significance. The pupil-teacher pattern of our formal schooling days is no longer relevant. As trainers we are challenged to create a conducive learning climate by using a variety of methods to suit different learning styles.

Any learning experience provided through training should be organised with the *learning principles for adults* firmly in mind. Nine key principles are as follows. The adult learns best:

1 when he or she takes part actively;
2 when learning concerns problems he or she is interested in and encounters in every day life;
3 when learning is useful and practical;
4 if he or she receives feedback;
5 if he or she is given encouragement and reinforcement;
6 when he or she has an opportunity to utilise his or her knowledge, ability and skills in a variety of situations;
7 if he or she feels free to say when and how he or she is having problems;
8 when conflicts and frustrations are resolved;
9 if treated with sincerity, justice and in a reasonable way.

Some of the techniques of two trainers with distinctive training styles are described overleaf. Keeping in mind the learning principles for adults we invite you to examine each technique and select those which you consider will promote maximum learning opportunities for adults.

The two columns of training techniques outlined here clearly differentiate the trainer using a participatory style (left hand column) from

The trainer:	*The trainer:*
• designs the curriculum based on an analysis of tasks, needs and expectations of trainees.	• designs the curriculum based on his assessment of goals to be achieved.
• involves the trainee in creation and revision of programme objectives, and/or the identification of individual learning needs and objectives related to where the trainee is and wants to go.	• defines objectives for trainee achievement at the beginning of the programme; holds to these throughout to maintain consistency and coherence.
• assists trainees in identifying possible learning activities and in effectively structuring such activities.	• decides what learning activities are most appropriate and expects trainees to follow this structure.
• expects the trainee to learn by exploration and discovery, making use of available resources, and solving problems.	• expects the trainee to learn primarily by absorbing material through lectures, reading, etc., by memorising or practice and by responding to trainer questions.
• involves the trainees in decision making; invites ideas, suggestions and criticism from the trainees.	• makes the decisions or carries out the decisions made by staff; does not invite suggestions or criticism from the trainees.
• structures the training so that unplanned and unexpected problems will be treated as learning opportunities.	• follows the schedule closely; avoids problems or dispenses with them quickly so that they will not interfere with the planned sequence or schedule.
• promotes cooperative work among trainees and a climate of openness, trust and concern for others.	• promotes individual learning efforts, accountability and competition among trainees.
• promotes self-assessment by trainees, and provides feedback of information needed by trainees to evaluate their own progress.	• personally assesses trainee performance and progress, usually through formal tests.
• involves the trainees in mid-course or final evaluation of the training programme, process, materials and its progress towards achieving objectives, and elicits suggestions.	• does own mid course or final evaluation of training programme and its effectiveness; draws own conclusions about needed revisions.

that using a directive style (right hand column). The application of some of the general principles and techniques of participative training were described in the account of the Banjarnegara training programme in the previous chapter.

Once you have reached a decision on the training style most appropriate in your situation it is your task as a trainer to design all the learning experiences in your training programme - whether it be for volunteer health workers, paramedics, field workers or others - to fit as closely as possible with that style. We trust that you will join us in opting wholeheartedly for the participative style as the most appropriate to enable maximum adult learning.

The exercises – maximising their use

In the remaining chapters of this book we present a variety of structured exercises. They are just one of the many tools which can be used by the trainers to promote the active participation of trainees in the learning process. As with most participatory methods, these exercises are based on the concept of experiential learning, or learning from an experience. Experiential learning is a spontaneous part of everyone's daily life. Constantly we engage in an activity, look back at it critically, abstract some useful insight from our analysis of what happened, and then put the result into practice.

In the training situation we endeavour to create or simulate an experience. It may be in the form of a game, a role play, story or written case study. Such exercises are used as a basis for *commencing* the inductive learning process. It is important for the trainer to be aware that an exercise, however dynamic or stimulating, is rarely, by itself, a learning experience. Therefore it is the *trainer's task to develop the exercise into a complete learning experience together with the trainees.* The complete process can be illustrated as follows:

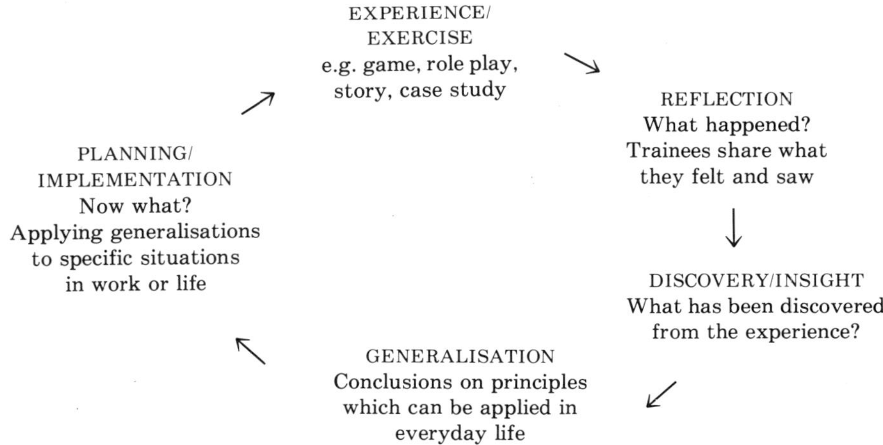

EXPERIENCE → REFLECTION → DISCOVERY - these three steps are related to the *experience/exercise* itself.

The experience/exercise is only the beginning. The following steps are *much more important* than the simulated experience.

GENERALISATION → PLANNING IMPLEMENTATION - these two steps are related to *every day experience.*

The trainer should complete the experiential learning cycle with discussion on the *implementation* or *application* of the generalisations in the trainees work and life situation. What can be done in my situation to apply these principles? Should I make changes in my situation? If so, what changes? To facilitate this process the trainees could be requested to give examples of similar situations occurring in their life situation, or a strategy for the implementation of the principles could be developed by the trainees in small groups.

Selecting the most appropriate exercise

The most important factors to take into consideration when selecting an exercise are:

- the learning goals to be achieved, i.e. the trainees' learning needs;
- the trainer's competence in facilitating the exercise.

Other factors which may need to be taken into account include:

- the time available for the exercise;
- the number of trainees;
- the trainees' past experience;
- required materials;
- space available.

The exercises are presented in the approximate order in which they may be introduced in a training course to build the sensitivity and confidence of the group. There are a couple of exceptions. To help the trainer, we list below the various stages of a training programme and give the number of the exercise which can be used at each stage.

Stage I	Introducing group members - exercises 1,2,3,4.
Stage II	Planning the training with participants - exercises 5,7.
Stage III	Forming groups - exercises 6,8,22,23.
Stage IV	Discovering communication problems - exercises 9,10,11, 12,15,16,17.
Stage V	Developing good communications among groups - exercises 13,14,24.
Stage VI	Developing group work skills - exercises 18,19,20,21.
Stage VII	Developing team work skills - exercises 22,23,24,25.
Stage VIII	Developing leadership skills - exercises 26,27,28,29.
Stage IX	Developing planning skills - exercises 7,30,31,32,33,34,35, 36,37,38.
Stage X	Using planning simulation exercises - exercises 39,40,41.

Preparing the exercises

Each exercise is systematically explained starting with the purpose and proceeding to the objectives, the time required for the exercise, the type of place and the materials needed. A step by step guide to the activity is presented. Finally, suggestions about how to develop the discussion and conclusions are given. These suggestions, in many cases, include a number of questions which have proved useful in stimulating discussion. In some exercises, we have noted problems which might occur during or as a result of the exercise.

Concerning materials you will need, most exercises require little more than felt pens, writing pens or pencils and boards or paper on which to write down ideas. When other materials are needed, such as a specific picture or form, they have been placed on a separate page in order that the material can be reproduced fairly easily.

Examples which we use for case studies are based on reality but obviously do not reflect the local situation. Trainers are therefore encouraged to adapt these materials to reflect their own environment. In this way it will be much easier for trainees to identify with the problems and to be more enthusiastic about seeking solutions.

To summarise, in the following chapters each exercise includes:

1 the purpose of the exercise;
2 the specific objectives;
3 time - how long it takes;
4 place - how large a space;
5 materials - pens, paper, posters etc.;
6 the activity - information on the steps for creating an experience;
7 discussion - questions to facilitate the process of reflection and discovery of insight;
8 conclusions - generalisations which can be drawn from the experience.

Suggested do's and don't's

Below are some hints to assist you in increasing your competence in presenting the structured exercises.[1]

Do

Prepare

- Work out the sequence of events which should take place.
- Check the timing.
- Have materials, handouts, etc. ready.

Plan alternatives

- Have some other activity prepared in case the group is already familiar with the exercise, or is either more or less experienced than expected.

Set up the situation

- Give a broad overview first.
- Give instructions one by one.
- Always keep the purpose of the exercise in mind.

Facilitate the process

- Give everyone something to do at all times (taking part, observing etc.).
- Let the group help you.

1 For these hints we have borrowed heavily from J. William Pfeiffer and John E. Jones, (Eds.), *A Handbook of Structured Experiences for Human Relations Training*, Vol. II, San Diego, CA: University Associates, Inc., 1974.

Facilitate learning

- Turn everything that happens into learning.
- Help the participants apply what they learn.

Don't

Overinstruct

- Give too much detail.
- Explain in advance what will probably happen.
- Tell too much rather than listening.
- Force people to participate.

Force your interpretation

- Argue over interpretations of what happened.
- Defend your own views of what should happen.
- Stress individual psychological interpretations.

Overload

- Generate more data than can be discussed.
- Repeat an activity until it 'works right'.
- Over analyse data.

End without a structured ending

- Leave people on their own to solve problems.
- Leave application to chance.

Now it is over to you. Enjoy yourself.

4 *Working together: group formation skills*

Early in a course the major function of the trainer is to create a favourable climate between both trainees and trainers to begin the process of getting to know each other. Good introductions begin a mutual exchange which in turn encourages frankness. This frankness is basic capital for the formation of a strong group, a major requirement for successful interactive learning. It is clear that the more comfortable the participants feel with one another, the greater the chances of developing a learning environment that welcomes new ideas and stimulates growth. Each trainee will also find it easier to express what they hope to obtain from the training. It is also forseen that the trainees will begin to gain greater confidence in expressing themselves and in sharing with a group. These skills will be a valuable asset in their contact and work with community groups.

The introductory exercises given in this section are non-threatening because they leave it open to trainees to choose how much personal information they wish to share with the group.

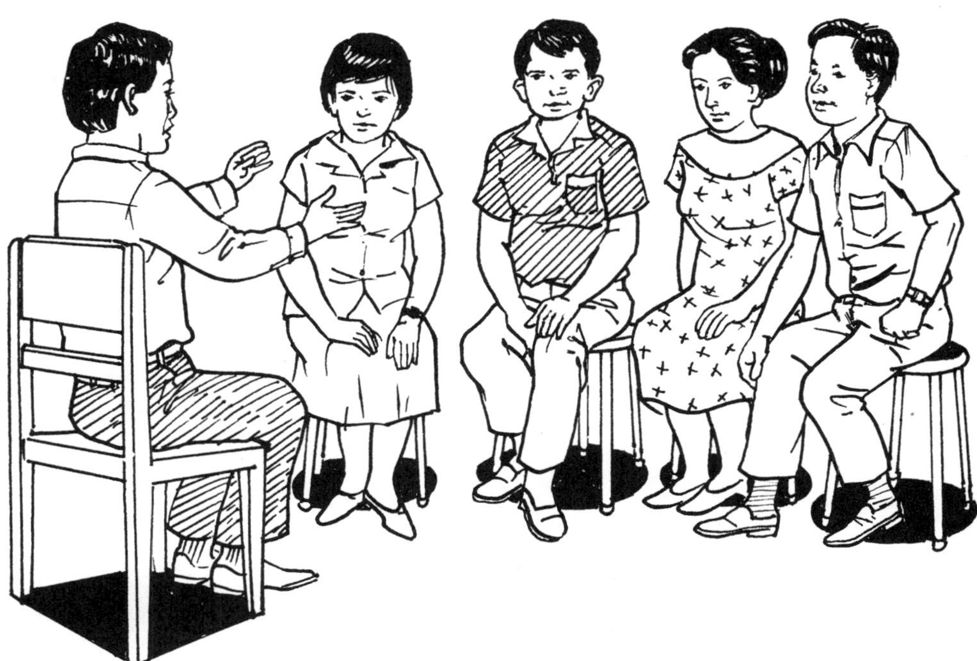

The material can be used by the trainer to help lay the foundations for the formation of a strong group and a basis for developing a group cohesiveness.

It should be kept in mind, however, that group formation is an on-going process which will not be completed within the first stage of a course but must be actively encouraged throughout the whole training.

1 Using name cards

Purpose

Participants often not only do not know one another but also come from different places and backgrounds.

This exercise is one that can be used to begin the process of getting to know each other.

Objectives

1 The participants will know a few basic facts about each other.
2 The participants will begin to take an active part in the group.

Time

30-40 minutes

Place

A room or place sufficiently large for people to move around

Materials

Empty cards (7 × 10 cm) for each person
Ballpoint pens or pencils
A glass, bottle, box or hat

The activity

Introduction
Explain to the participants the rules of the game and the steps described below.

Steps
1 Give each participant an empty card.
2 Ask each participant to write the following on his or her card:
- complete name;
- name of organisation;
- his or her tasks/work in the organisation.

3 After all the cards are completed, collect them and mix them together. Place them in a container and invite each participant to take one card from the container ensuring that the participant does not have his or her own card.
4 After each participant has one card, instruct the person to find the owner of the card. Then ask each person to find out more information about the owner.
5 After five minutes ask everyone to be seated and ask each person to introduce the owner of the card which he or she has picked.

Discussion and conclusions

On completion of the introductions invite the participants to share their feelings during this exercise.

Points which can be emphasised

1 A more friendly atmosphere has been achieved now because all participants have begun to know each other.

2 It is now easier for the participants to communicate with each other.

3 It is not easy to introduce someone else because we must make sure that we do not upset the feelings of the person we are introducing, or misrepresent them.

2 Playing another's role

Purpose

In some cases, some participants know each other and some do not. This exercise is to introduce all participants to each other and to help each participant to know other participants better.

Objectives

1 Each participant will be able to mention the name, work and hobbies of other participants.

2 Each participant may begin to be aware of the points of view of other people.

Time

60 minutes (this may be longer if there are a large number of participants)

Place

Large enough for all participants

Materials

None

The activity

Introduction
Explain the objective of personal introductions and what participants are expected to do in this exercise.

Steps
1 Divide participants into pairs.
2 Ask each pair to spend 10 minutes learning about each other.
3 Ask each pair to introduce themselves to the other participants in the following way:
• Each member of the pair introduces him or herself as if he or she were the other member of the pair.

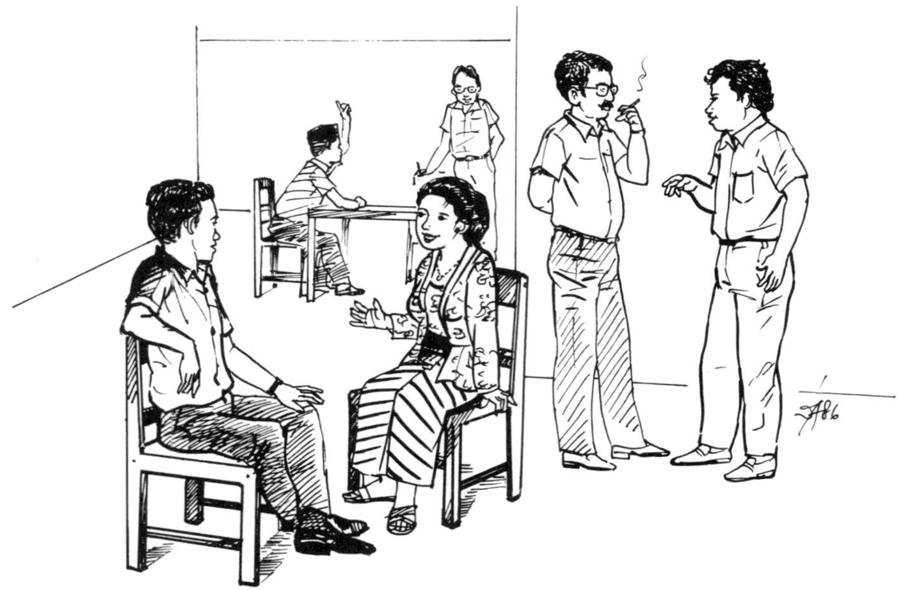

• For example, A introduces herself as if she were B and B introduces himself as if he were A.
4 Ask all pairs to use this method of introduction.
5 If there is sufficient time allow other participants to ask questions of the person introducing 'her or himself'.

Discussion and conclusions

Discussion
The following points might be discussed with the participants:
• how it feels to act as another person;
• how it feels if our role is played by someone else, particularly if the person misrepresents us.

Points which can be emphasised
1 It is difficult to be completely free of our own concerns and fully appreciate another person.

2 It is more difficult to get to know the attitudes and habits of someone than to get to know his or her name.
3 It is a long term process to get to know attitudes and habits of other people.

3 Who fits the description?

Purpose

This exercise has the same purpose and objectives as Exercise 2.

Objectives

The same as Exercise 2

Time

30-40 minutes

Materials

The same as Exercise 2
Cards - the same number as the number of participants and trainer(s). Each card has a hobby or personal characteristic written on it, e.g. 'is a member of a choir', 'likes dancing'. This exercise requires sensitivity. It is perhaps best to ask participants to write positive characteristics on the card.
A container such as a bottle, hat, box etc.

The activity

Introduction
Explain to the participants the steps which are described below.

Steps
1 Invite each participant to take one card. Take one card yourself.
2 Tell each person to select the person who most closely fits the description on the card.
3 Ask each person to find out about the person he or she has selected.

4 After 10 minutes ask everyone to be seated and ask each person to introduce the person he or she chose. Explain also why he or she linked the characteristics on the card.

On completion of the introductions invite the participants to share their feelings during this exercise.

Discussion and conclusions

Points which can be emphasised

1 A more friendly atmosphere has begun to be achieved because all participants have shared some personal concern with another person.

2 First impressions can sometimes be misleading.

3 It is now easier to communicate with each other.

4 Likes or dislikes

Purpose

The group has just met and not everyone knows all members of the group. This exercise is to enable everyone in the group to know something about each group member.

Objectives

1 The participants will know each others names and a few characteristics about each other.

2 The participants will begin to feel relaxed in the group.

Time

Approximately 40 minutes for a group of 20 people

Place

Any place where the participants can sit together

Materials

None

The activity

Introduction

Explain briefly how introductions take place.

Steps

1 Introduce yourself to the person sitting next to you saying. 'My name is ... and I like ...'. The object or activity which you claim you like should begin with the same letter as your name, e.g. 'My name is Tom and I like Tomatoes'.

2 The second person then introduces him or herself to a third person saying: 'My name is ... and I like ...'. He or she then adds: 'And this is ... and he or she likes ...' (referring to the first person, i.e. the trainer).

3 This process is continued until the last person is reached. Each person must repeat the names and the likes of all the people introduced before him or her.

4 If the group is more than 10 people, begin the process again at number 11.

Discussion and conclusions

Discussion
On completion ask the group if they find it easier to remember a name if they link the name with a particular characteristic of the person.

Points which can be emphasised
1 This is the beginning of a 'getting-to-know-you' process.
2 Through this experience we have learned about several characteristics of each person, not only through words but also through their actions.

Variations

The trainer can suggest that participants mention a hobby, a dislike or some other characteristic as an alternative to 'likes'.

5 Identifying participants' expectations

Purpose

At the beginning of the training course the trainers wish to know what the participants expect from the course in order that they can present a curriculum which tries to meet the needs of the participants. Through this exercise it is hoped that:

Objectives

1 The participants share their expectations on training methods and content.
2 The participants can learn what other participants hope to gain from the course.

Time

90 minutes

Place

A quiet area with space for participants to write

Materials

Writing paper
Large sheets of paper
Felt pens

The activity

Introduction
Explain the desire of the trainers to adjust the content of the course to the needs of the participants.

Steps
1 Ask each participant to write down what she or he expects from the training.
2 Divide the participants into small groups of three to four people to discuss together the hopes of each member of the group and to combine their hopes as a group.
3 Ask each small group to write their expectations on large sheets of paper.

4 Attach the large sheets to the wall and read aloud the expectations to the whole group.

NOTE: The trainer(s), in the interest of time, may collect the expectations of each participant and after categorising them, display them on the white sheets of paper on the wall.

Discussion and conclusions

Discussion
The trainer/participants can ask for information about expectations which are not clearly expressed. The trainer could explain which expectations cannot be met during the training programme and why. The trainer explains also that the combined expectations are the expectations of the whole group. They can only be met if both the trainers and the participants work together to achieve them.

Variation A

If the participants have difficulty in expressing their expectations because of a low educational level, limited experience, or lack of understanding of what they must do, they can be helped in the following way.

Before drawing up expectations request the participants to list the problems which they face in their environment. Based on these problems ask them to state what they would like to gain from the training to help them overcome such problems.

Variation B

If the participants have been requested to write down their expectations during the preparatory phases of the course, all the expectations can be organised in a list by the trainer. This list can then be given to the participants in small groups. Ask each group to discuss these questions.

- Does the list reflect their expectations?

- Does the group want to eliminate or add to the list?

Discuss the results in the complete group.

Variation C

If the trainer wants to link up expectations with the functions which the participants will be expected to carry out after the training ask each participant to make a list of their functions or tasks. Request them to write down the knowledge, skills and attitudes they need to perform these tasks effectively.

For example:

Tasks	*Knowledge*	*Skills*	*Attitudes*
To give information for breast-feeding	Why and how to breastfeed	How to speak well	Open, sensitive, informative

Then ask the participants to write down the knowledge, skills and attitudes which they feel they still need to master in order to perform their tasks. These notes are the expectations of the participants.

Variation D

Each participant finds another participant who he or she does not yet know. Each pair is given the chance to discuss together for three minutes:

- what they hope to obtain from the training experience;
- any fears or worries they have about the training.

After six minutes the whole group meets again. Each pair reports their hopes and fears. The trainer gives each pair a chance to improve their report if they so desire. The trainer writes up the results systematically on a large sheet of paper.

A more complete picture can be obtained if each participant is requested to fill in the following framework.

My expectation	What I can contribute
Problems of being with me	My hopes toward other participants and facilities

MOST IMPORTANT

If the participants have been asked to draw up their expectations the trainers must make a special effort to endeavour to fulfil these expectations or address the question of why fulfilment was not possible. If the trainer does not treat participant expectations seriously the participants will be disappointed and it may affect their morale during training.

6 A meaningful article

Purpose

At the beginning of the training the participants have begun to get to know each other but their knowledge of each other is still superficial. Through this exercise it is hoped that:

Objectives

1 The participants are willing to be open about themselves.
2 The participants indicate their willingness to get to know the other participants.
3 The participants understand their relationship within the group.

Time

45–60 minutes

Place

Sufficient for all participants

Materials

Large sheets of paper
Felt pens for each group
Drawing pins to attach paper to walls/blackboard

The activity

Introduction
There are many different ways of getting to know others. This is one of them.

Steps
1 Invite each participant to look for something which is meaningful to him or her in the immediate environment.
2 Ask the participants to collect in small groups (four to five people) to tell the others why the article they have chosen is important to them and in what way. The group then can draw a conclusion about their impressions.

3 A plenary session is held to hear the conclusions of each small group and draw a conclusion to cover the whole group. The group can ask questions if points are not clear.

Discussion and conclusions

Points which can be emphasised
1 Sometimes it is difficult for a participant to express his or her feelings about the chosen object. Someone in the group can help by asking appropriate questions.
2 The small group may also have difficulty in drawing a conclusion about the sum total of their experience.
3 It often happens that two participants choose the same object, but rarely do they choose it for the same reason.

7 Picturing one's role or function

Purpose

At the beginning of a course the trainer will probably wish to know how the participants perceive their role or function in their everyday work, or the role or function they will perform on the completion of the training. At the end of the course, the trainer and participants will probably wish to know whether their perceptions have changed.

Objectives

1 Each participant can present their role or function in pictorial form.
2 Each participant has a deeper understanding of his or her role and that of the other participants.

Time

30-45 minutes

Place

Sufficient space for all the participants to draw pictures

Materials

A piece of paper of approximately 35 cm square for each participant
Felt pens
Drawing pins to attach the drawings to the wall

The activity

Introduction
Ask the participants to draw their role or function in their everyday work. They may draw a realistic picture or use symbols. For example, if the trainees are a group of nurses each participant is asked to draw her role as a nurse.

Steps
1 Divide the paper between the participants.
2 Ask each participant to draw his or her role.
3 Attach the drawings to the walls.
4 Repeat the above steps at the end of the course.

Discussion and conclusions

Invite the participants to look at each others' drawings. If anything is not clear, trainers may ask the owner of the picture to discuss it. It is better that the trainer does not make an analysis although he or she may wish to make comments.

After participants do the drawings at the end of the course (using the same instructions), the participants can be invited to:

- compare the first and second drawings;
- explain the differences in his or her drawings to the other participants.

By using this exercise at the beginning and end of a course the trainer and participants can evaluate the influence of the training by comparing the change in concept of role or function.

8 Forming working groups

Purpose

During the training the participants may have to work in groups over a period. This exercise gives the opportunity to divide themselves into groups rather than being divided by the trainer(s). It is hoped that:

Objectives

The participants can form groups with people with whom they wish to work.

Time

30 minutes

Place

In the classroom

Materials

A small piece of paper for each participant
Blackboard or white board with the following writing on it:

Group A   Group B   Group C

Drawing pins

The activity

Introduction

Explain many learning activities require group work. Rather than having the course trainer choose these groups, it is better for the trainees to select their own group members. Ask the participants to choose these groups following these simple conditions:

- the size of the groups are the same;
- preferably people from the same organisation are in different groups;
- preferably each group has members with a variety of skills.

Steps

1 Ask each participant to write his or her name, name of organisation and special skills on a piece of paper.

2 Ask each participant to attach his or her piece of paper in the column indicating the group he or she would like to be in, taking into account the conditions given above.

3 If the groups are not evenly divided invite the participants to make the needed adjustments.

Discussion and conclusions

Conclusion

Usually the participants are pleased with their group because they have had the opportunity to select their own group. If they have to work for several sessions in this group usually the group works well together.

5 Talking together (1): communication skills

Communication is familiar to us all. From birth, or even before, we have communicated with those in our immediate environment and beyond. However, because of its very familiarity we often pay little attention to how effectively we communicate with others. For community workers sensitive, fluent communication will be the key to effective work. Consensus seeking, problem solving and non verbal interaction are just a few of the communication skills which they will need to master. They will also possess valuable tools if they understand the factors which support and hinder good communication.

Ease of communication is no less important in the training situation. It is a major element achieving togetherness and open, sympathetic and tolerant sharing during a course. Communication is thus an important

topic which should be covered in every training, preferably during the early stages. This will enable the exercises and discussion to be used to help promote group formation and initiate the process of acquiring the knowledge, attitudes and skills needed by an effective community worker.

Participatory methodology - such as group discussions, role play and games - is ideal for testing out new or improved methods of communicating. It is possible for all transactions throughout the training to be oriented to the sharpening of communication skills, and therefore the development of such skills should be the concern of all trainers involved in the training process.

9 Distortion in communication

Purpose

During the training it is likely that communication problems will arise among the participants and between the participants and the trainer. The purpose of this group of exercises is to enable the participants to be more open and gain more understanding of factors which give rise to communication problems during the training and in the community. *For this reason it is useful to discuss this subject in the first days of the course.*

There are several ways to lead into discussion on distortions in communication. The exercises which are suggested here hope that:

Objectives

1 The participants understand some of the factors which hinder good communication.
2 The participants understand some of the factors which promote good communication.
3 The participants can communicate more effectively.

Exercise A

Time

30 minutes

Place

Classroom

Materials

A piece of paper for each participant
Pen, pencils or felt pens for each participant
Blackboard or large piece of paper

The activity

Introduction
In the process of communication, explain that the sender of a message (or the speaker) always hopes that the receiver of the message (or the listener) receives the same message as he has sent. Give examples. Then you can ask: 'But is the process of communication as easy as this?'

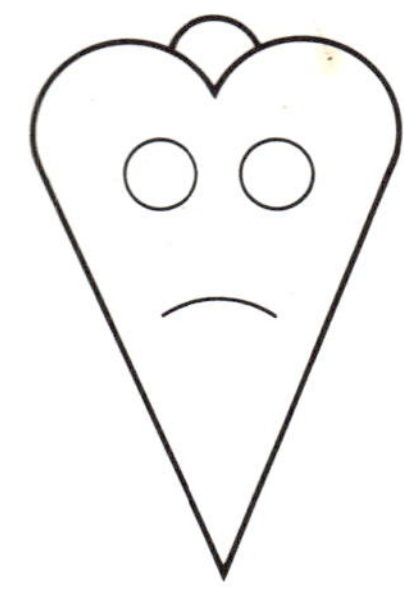

Steps

1 Draw a simple picture like the one shown on a large piece of paper or on the blackboard.

2 Show the picture to all the participants. When all have seen it, remove the picture.

3 Repeat briefly the process of communication.

4 Then ask the participants to draw the same picture they saw on a piece of paper.

5 Show the pictures to all the participants, or ask several participants to repeat their picture on the blackboard.

6 Note the differences in the drawings by comparing them with the original.

Discussion and conclusions

Points which can be emphasised

It will be found that most of the participants have drawn a picture which is not exactly the same as the original one.

From this we can draw the conclusion that problems can occur even when the communication is direct and simple.

If the message is more complicated or if it is given by other people or the media, there are even greater chances of problems or distortions.

Despite the best of intentions, distortions can happen, as we saw in the case of the simple drawings.

If there are bad intentions, the chances of distortion are so much greater. For example, if we want to spread rumours about someone, it is easy to distort the real situation. Ask the participants to give other examples.

Exercise B

Time — 15 minutes

Place — Classroom

Materials — Blackboard or large piece of paper

The activity

Introduction

Explain that often problems in life can be seen in many different ways. Therefore we should always examine others' opinions, especially when they differ from our opinion, even though we are convinced our opinion is right.

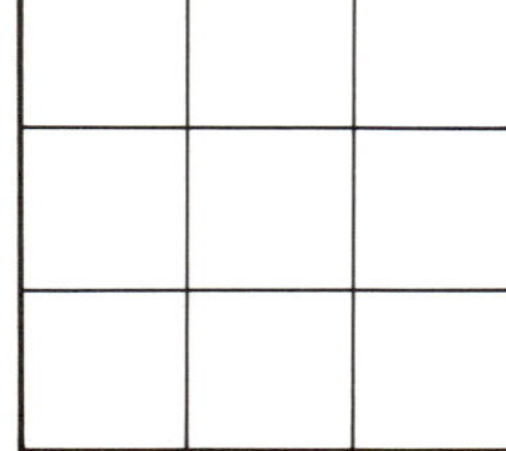

Steps

1 Draw a picture like the one shown on the blackboard or paper.

2 Ask the participants how many squares there are.

3 The participants will probably give a variety of answers such as 9, 10, 14. Each is acceptable.

Discussion and conclusions

Points which can be emphasised

Examine with the participants the differences in the answers. Each person will believe he or she is right. Ask people with different answers to explain how they reached a particular number.

You can conclude that in every day life we should always try to understand the opinions and way of thinking of other people, including the basis for their way of thinking.

NOTE: This exercise is particularly effective if it is used when a heated argument occurs and neither side is prepared to listen to or consider each other's opinion.

---

10 One-way communication

Purpose

The participants require communication skills so that they can participate effectively in the training and carry out their tasks in the community successfully. Therefore it is important that the participants become aware of the advantages of two-way communication in the early stages of the training. Through this exercise it is hoped that:

Objectives

1 The participants know the inadequacies of one-way communication.
2 The participants understand that two-way communication is essential.

Time

45 minutes

Place

An area large enough for participants to move about

Materials

Five large pieces of paper, drawing pins, felt pens
Picture with a clear, simple health message, illustration on page 32 is an example

The activity

Introduction

Explain the process of communication using examples, e.g. in the family, the community, work groups etc.

Steps

1 Ask five participants to take part in this exercise. Ask the other participants to observe the process.
2 Ask the five participants to number off from one to five.
3 Ask No. 2 to No. 5 to leave the room.

NOTE: No. 2 to No. 5 should not be able to see or hear what is going on in the classroom.

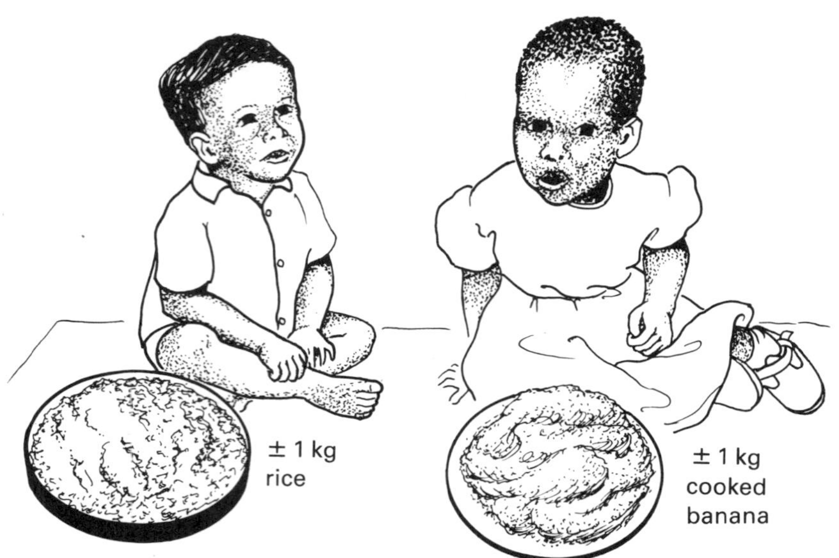

The volume a child has to eat to consume 1000 calories

4 a) Show a health message to No. 1, also show the picture to the observers, then put the picture aside.

b) Ask No. 2 to come into the classroom.

c) Ask No. 1 to explain the picture to No. 2 who is expected to draw it on the large piece of paper attached to the blackboard or wall, according to the instructions from No. 1. While giving the instructions, No. 1 has his back to No. 2. No. 2 is not allowed to ask questions.

d) On completion ask No. 1 to sit down again.

e) Put aside the picture made by No. 2.

f) Call No. 3 into the classroom.

g) No. 2 gives instructions to No. 3 to draw the picture on another piece of paper.

h) On completion ask No. 2 to sit down again.

i) Put aside the picture made by No. 2.

j) Complete the process when all five participants have drawn the picture.

5 Show the original picture and all the pictures from No. 1 to No. 5 to everyone.

Discussion and conclusions

Points which can be emphasised

What do you think of the results? Are they the same?

Why are they not the same?

You can look for the reasons for the discrepancies from the participants, and note them down on the blackboard.

In one-way communication there are many inadequacies. You can list all the inadequacies which were revealed by the exercise. See page 34 for some examples.

11 Two-way communication

Purpose

We still often come across one-way communication in the community, for example, orders, either written or oral, delivered in an atmosphere in which discussion or questions are impossible. Health education talks which do not invite questions are another example.

Experience has proved that one-way communication has many weaknesses, which can be overcome if the communication becomes two-way. Therefore, through this exercise it is hoped that:

Objectives

1 The participants are aware of the weaknesses of one-way communication.
2 The participants are aware of and accept the superiority of two-way communication.

Time

60–75 minutes

Materials

A drawing of approximately 30–40 cm
At least one piece of folio sized paper for each participant
Blackboard and chalk
An example: see illustration below.

The activity

Introduction
Give a few examples of one-way and two-way communication, then explain the rules of the exercise.

Steps
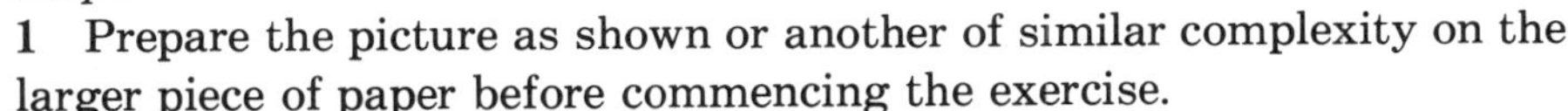
1 Prepare the picture as shown or another of similar complexity on the larger piece of paper before commencing the exercise.
2 Place the picture in a position where it can be seen by the participants who are standing, but is not visible to the participants who are sitting down.
3 The participants are requested to sit in a circle and then number off 1 and 2 until the whole group is divided into 2 groups. Each No. 1 remains seated, with about 2 metres between each chair. Each No. 2 is requested to stand at the back of his or her No. 1.
4 All No. 2's are requested to walk slowly past the picture.
5 They return to their partners standing once more behind the chair. Each No. 2 then gives instructions to his or her No. 1 partner to draw the picture exactly as he describes it. He or she then explains the picture in detail. No. 1 attempts to draw, according to the instructions of No. 2, on a piece of paper. No. 1 is not allowed to talk. No. 2 is not permitted to look at the original picture again while drawing.
6 When the picture is completed, it should be marked 'A'. No. 2. is requested to walk slowly past the picture again. He or she should then return to his or her partner and once again give instructions on how to

draw the picture. No. 1 makes a second drawing. If any point is unclear, the drawer may ask questions. This picture is marked 'B'.

7 On completion of the second picture the participants are asked to compare the two pictures, and then compare them with the original picture which is displayed by the trainer.

Discussion and conclusions

On comparing the two pictures you can ask the following questions.

1 Which picture is best?

2 Why is the second picture best?

3 To No. 1: How did you feel when you had to draw but were not allowed to speak?

4 To No. 2: How did you feel when you had to give instructions but were not allowed to help your partner in any other way?

5 Which type of communication was most effective, the first or the second?

6 What are the advantages of two-way communication?

The following conclusions may be drawn:

1 Two-way communication is more effective than one-way communication.

2 Two-way communication is easier for the recipient to accept and to understand.

3 Two-way communication is able to eliminate suspicion, disappointment, apathy and other negative feelings.

4 Two-way communication is able to provide immediate feedback.

12 Two-way communication (2)

Purpose

We still often come across one-way communication in the community. For example, orders, either written or oral, delivered in an atmosphere in which discussion or questions are impossible. Health education talks which do not invite questions are another example. Experience has proved that one-way communication has many weaknesses, which can be overcome if communication becomes two-way. Therefore through this exercise it is hoped that:

Objectives

1 The participants are aware of the weaknesses of one-way communication.

2 The participants can explain in what ways two-way communication is superior.

Time

60 minutes

Place

Classroom

Materials

Two blackboards and chalk, or two flipcharts and felt pens
A picture

The activity

Introduction

Give several examples of one-way and two-way communication. Then explain that shortly the participants are going to be involved in both one-way and two-way communication.

Steps

1 Place two blackboards in front of the group, in such a way that the two people who will be drawing on them cannot see each others' drawing.
2 Select one communicator and four recipients. Ask the other participants to observe the process closely.
3 Ask the four recipients to leave the room and explain to the observers that the communicator is going to give instructions to two recipients to draw the same picture.
4 Ask observers to observe the whole process, including the behaviour of the communicator and each of the recipients. Tell the observers that they are not allowed to speak or assist in any way.
5 Give the picture to the communicator and tell him or her to study it for ±2 minutes.
6 Request two of the recipients to return to the classroom. Tell them to draw the picture which the communicator describes. Inform them that they are not allowed to look at each others pictures or to ask questions.
7 Ask the communicator to stand with his or her back to the recipients. He or she also is not allowed to look at the blackboard.
8 Ask the communicator to give instructions to the two recipients on how to draw the picture which he or she saw.

9 The recipients draw on their respective blackboards according to the instructions of the communicator. If drawn on a blackboard the two pictures are copied and put away for the time being.
10 Follow the same process for the other two recipients. But this time allow the communicator to face the blackboards and to repeat his instructions if needed. The recipients may also ask questions.
11 Compare the four pictures.

Discussion and conclusions

You can ask the participants if the pictures are the same. Why are the results different? Ask for the reasons for the differences from the communicator, the recipients, and the observers. Make a list of reasons why the pictures are different.

Points which can be emphasised
1 If a message is given in an atmosphere which does not enable feedback, the recipient will interpret it according to his own background.
2 Two-way communication is superior because it is quicker and more easily understood by the recipient. Many misunderstandings and distortions can be avoided.

Exercise adapted, with permission, from
From the Field: Tested Participatory Activities for Trainers, compiled by Catherine D. Crone and Carman St. John Hunter, New York: World Education, 1980.

13 A trio of listeners

Purpose

In implementing tasks in the community the participants will need skills in listening to others and putting appropriate questions to them. It is not enough to just hear words. They will also need to listen with full attention with their minds and hearts.

Objectives

1 The participants understand the meaning of listening.
2 The participants are aware of the necessity of listening to each other.
3 The participants understand the factors which hinder us from listening carefully to others.

Time

45 minutes

Place

A place wide enough to enable each trio to chat without disturbing other trios

The activity

Introduction
Emphasise the importance of listening carefully to others. Explain the exercise.

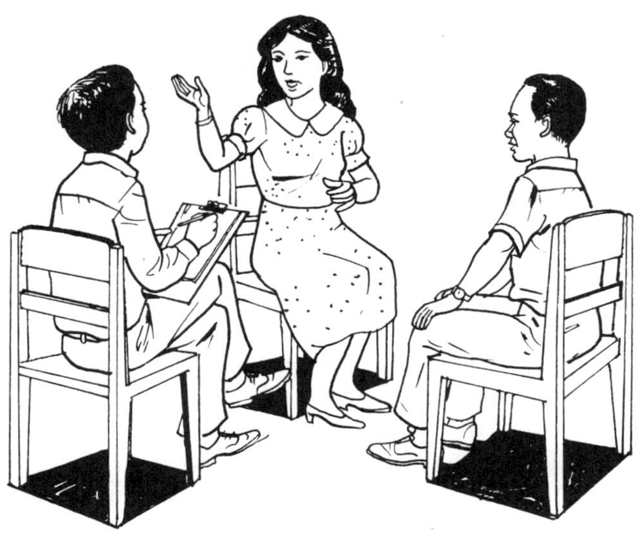

Steps

1 Divide the participants into groups of three.
2 Give each member of the group a code number: A,B,C.

A = listener
B = speaker
C = judge/observer

3 Ask each group to select a topic of conversation or suggest a topic.
4 B opens the discussion. A listens, then repeats *in essence* what he or she has just heard before responding to B. C observes and corrects any mistakes (if necessary).
5 Continue discussion for about seven minutes using the method outlined in 4.
6 After finishing the discussion put the questions given below and ask each participant to answer. This takes 15 minutes.
7 Ask group members to change their functions:

A = speaker
B = judge/observer
C = listener

8 After B has had seven minutes change again with C as the speaker.
9 After all members of the group have had the opportunity to play all the roles again put the questions to all participants. This can be in written form or oral.

Discussion and conclusions

1 You may ask several participants to read out or give their answers. Before discussing each answer ask if any other participant has a different answer. If this is the case ask for their answer for extra material for discussion.
2 From their answers you can put together a list of factors which make it difficult for us to listen carefully to others.

Questions for discussion

1 Did you find it difficult to listen to your friend? Why?

2 Did you find it difficult to organise your thinking while also trying to listen?

- Did you forget what you wanted to say?
- Did you find it hard to hear what was said?
- Did you prepare your answer and repeat it to yourself?

3 When your friend repeated the essence of what you said was it shorter than what you had said? Was it complete?

4 Did you feel that what you wanted to say was not received clearly by the listener?

5 Did the way your friend spoke influence your ability to listen well? Compare the two people who spoke.

In conclusion, you can emphasise the factors which help us to be good listeners.

14 Repeating

Purpose

When communicating we hope that what we say is understood exactly by the person to whom we are talking. But in everyday life it often happens that what we say is understood differently from the way it was intended. One reason is that the ability of people to understand the essence of what another person is saying differs. Through this exercise it is hoped that:

Objectives

1 The participants evaluate their skill in understanding the essence of another person's conversation.

2 The participants increase their skill in understanding the essence of another person's conversation.

Time

30-45 minutes

Place

Classroom

Materials

None

The activity

Introduction

Explain the purpose of this exercise as described above.

Steps

1 Divide the participants into groups of from five to ten people. Note that the smaller the group the more intensive the exercise.

2 Ask the participants to number themselves off, 1,2,3,4, etc.

3 Instruct No. 1 to begin speaking to No. 2. If necessary suggest a topic of conversation. Stop the speaker after two to three minutes.

4 Before No. 2 responds to the conversation of No. 1, he or she must repeat the essence of No. 1's words until he or she is correct.
5 This process is repeated with No. 2 to No. 3, No. 3 to No. 4 until all the participants have a chance to repeat the essence of another's conversation.

Discussion and conclusions

You may discuss with the participants the factors which make it difficult to repeat the essence of another's conversation correctly.

Points which can be emphasised
1 In relation to the listener:
- could not hear well;
- afraid to question if not clear, etc.

2 In relation to the speaker:
- spoke too long;
- message was too complicated;
- voice was too soft;
- spoke too fast, etc.

You may conclude by pointing out that:
3 We will be a good listener if we:
- always concentrate our thoughts on the speaker;
- are prepared to question anything which is not clear;
- repeat anything which is difficult to check whether we have understood clearly.

4 We will be a good speaker if we:
- look at and pay attention to the listener;
- speak clearly and not monotonously;
- do not make our sentences too long;

- give the listener a chance to react and to ask questions;
- summarise or draw a conclusion at the end of our conversation etc.

NOTE: This exercise can be tried regularly throughout the training for a few minutes, e.g. before a session, to increase the participants' skill.

---

15 Creating a learning climate

Purpose

On some occasions the participants will have to function as trainers. The trainers must be able to communicate with the participants and use methods which can stimulate participation. Through this exercise it is hoped that:

Objectives

1 The participants can *explain* several ways of creating a good climate for learning.
2 The participants can *explain* the consequences of the trainer trying to force his or her own ideas upon the participants.

NOTE: It is suggested that this exercise only be used after the trainer and participants have been through a few sessions together under ordinary circumstances.

Time

60 minutes

Place

A room of sufficient size

Materials

Blackboard with chalk, or large pieces of paper and felt pens

The activity

Steps
1 Practice in advance so that you can carry through the exercise as naturally as possible. Study what must be said and done in Step 2. *Do not disclose to the group that you are only play acting.*

Follow these instructions:

- speak quickly;
- be gruff and unfriendly;
- go on regardless of the reactions of the participants.

2 Explain to the group that they are to be given a lesson on making a health poster (or something else appropriate in your circumstances). Be hard. Say to the group: 'Today we will discuss how to make a health poster. I trust that you will all participate in this discussion'.

Look at one participant and ask: 'Do you know how to make a poster?' Do not take any notice of his or her answer and do not react in any way. Look at someone else and ask the same question. Ignore his or her

answer. Then ask another person. 'Do you know what materials are used for making a poster?'

While he or she is giving his or her answer cut him or her off and say: 'Yes, yes we need a large piece of paper, some felt pens. Draw the message on a small draft paper before drawing it on the large paper. Write clearly. Make sure your picture is understood by all. Now does everyone understand how to make a health poster?'

Discussion and conclusions

Return to your usual way of speaking. Ask how the participants felt about the discussion and your way of presenting the material. Ask what you did right and what you did wrong. This question will make them aware that you were only play acting.

Points which can be emphasised

1 You can ask the group to present all the mistakes you made. You can ask one of the participants to write all the contributions on the blackboard.

2 Ask if adults can learn from the type of trainer you play acted? Ask their reactions in confronting a trainer like that.

3 The following points will probably be raised.

- You were unfriendly and frightening.
- You did not take any notice of the replies of the participants.
- Most of your questions only required a 'yes' or 'no' answer and did not invite discussion.
- You spoke too fast.
- The information and instructions were confusing.
- You claimed that paper and pens were needed but did not provide any.
- You did not show a poster and so the participants could not imagine what you were talking about.

4 You can then point out that all these factors hamper good communication.
5 In conclusion, you can point out that this demonstration is considered to be a good example of how not to give a lesson.

Exercises adapted, with permission, from *From the Field: Tested Participatory Activities for Trainers*, compiled by Catherine D. Crone and Carman St. John Hunter, New York: World Education, 1980.

16 Rumour clinic

Purpose

Misunderstandings often arise in communicating with others. If the participants understand the reasons for these misunderstandings they will be better prepared to try and communicate more effectively with others.

Objectives

1 The participants can explain how misunderstandings can arise in communicating with others.
2 The participants are aware of the importance of trying to avoid misunderstandings so that they can communicate more effectively with others.

Time

60-90 minutes

Place

Classroom and another room

Materials

A piece of paper with a message written on it
Blackboard and chalk
A piece of paper for each participant to write down the message they receive

The activity

Introduction
Give a brief explanation as above. Describe the exercise to the participants.

Steps
1 Make the following preparations:
- choose a message and write it on a piece of paper;
- make the message about five sentences long and about an event of significance to the participants;
- make the message disjointed, include figures, difficult words etc. (This is to obtain good feedback for discussion.)

2 Divide the participants into groups of five members. Each group member should sit about a metre away from the person next to him or her. Each group should be some distance from the other groups.

3 Ask each member of each group to count up to five.
4 Ask the No. 1 in each group to leave the room.
5 Join them outside the classroom and read the message to all the No. 1's twice. Do not allow participants to question you.
6 After hearing the message twice ask the No. 1's to join their group again and relay the message to No. 2 without the others hearing. Then No. 2 relays the message to No. 3 without the others hearing, and so on. The people receiving the message are not allowed to ask questions.
7 After receiving the message request each person to write down the message they relayed.
8 When all five members have heard the message request No. 5 to read out the message he or she received.
9 Read out the original message to all the participants.

Discussion and conclusions

Points which can be emphasised
You can ask the participants to compare the message they received with the original message. Note the changes together. Then ask the participants to suggest why these changes occurred.

This discussion can be noted on the blackboard as follows.

Message bearer	*Message receiver*	*Content of message*	*Method*
• voice unclear • impatient	• not concentrating • unable to hear	• too long • language difficult	• not allowed questions • not clear because whispered
• etc.	• etc.	• etc.	• no feedback • etc.

To stimulate answers the following questions can be asked:

- Could you receive the message clearly? If not, why?
- Did any message bearers add to or decrease the message? Why?
- Were you satisfied with the rules? If not, why?
- Did you think the message was organised systematically?

In conclusion, highlight that the factors which were noted down are those factors which often hamper good communication. If we reverse these factors we have a list of factors which promote good communication. Then give examples.

Variation

Steps

1 Choose five participants from the group.
2 Ask them to count from 1 to 5.
3 Ask Nos. 2,3,4 and 5 to wait outside.
4 Read the message to No. 1 twice.
5 Ask No. 2 to enter.
6 Request No. 1 to repeat the message he or she has just heard. The other participants must not assist.
7 Repeat this process until No. 5.
8 Read the original message to the group.
9 Conduct the discussion as outlined above.

The other participants can observe this process.

17 The perfect mimer

Purpose

In communicating with others misunderstandings often arise. If the participants understand the reasons for the misunderstandings they are more capable of trying to communicate more effectively with others.

Objectives

1 The participants can learn how misunderstandings arise in oral communication when passed from one person to another.
2 The participants are aware of the importance of trying to prevent misunderstandings so that they communicate more effectively.

Time

45-60 minutes

Place

Classroom

Materials

Blackboard and chalk

The activity

Introduction

Often there are discrepancies between the message which is conveyed and the message received. One reason is the difference in perception of the sender and the receiver.

Steps

1 Choose four extroverted participants, Nos. 2,3 and 4 are asked to leave the room.
2 Ask No. 1 to prepare him or herself to mime the actions of a complete activity, e.g. washing your hands before eating.
3 When No. 1 is ready call No. 2 to observe No. 1 perform the actions for 2 minutes.
4 Then call No. 3 to watch No. 2 repeat the actions of No. 1.
5 Then call No. 4 to observe No. 3 repeat the actions of No. 2.
6 Then No. 4 repeats the actions of No. 3.
7 Then No. 4 explains what he or she was doing. Ask No. 3 and No. 1 also to explain what they were doing.

Discussion and conclusions

Points which can be emphasised

1 a) The participants who observed can be asked to report on:

- any changes which occurred;
- any actions which were omitted;
- any additions which were made.

b) The reasons behind these distortions can be examined from the point of view of:

- the players (both sender and receiver);
- the way in which the message was conveyed;
- the content, that is the movements themselves.

2 All these factors can be drawn together and applied to emphasise that these are the reasons for distortions in chain communications. Examples can be used from the exercise just completed.

6 *Talking together (2): discussion skills*

A community development or community health worker will often find him or herself in a group involved in a discussion - either as a participant or as a facilitator. Therefore it is useful to be aware of how a good discussion should progress and to possess skills to facilitate the process.

This is equally true in the training setting where discussion groups are often used as a technique to gain maximum participation of the trainees. Often participants claim that discussion groups are one of the most beneficial experiences that they had during the training, particularly if the trainees come from a variety of backgrounds. It provides a forum where trainees can learn from each other by sharing their experiences.

To maximise the effectiveness of discussion groups it is often necessary to intervene with specific exercises to counteract negative tendencies, such as the domination of a discussion by one or two members, or the silence of a hesistant member. The following exercises will assist group members to be more aware of the importance of giving equal opportunities to all members to express their opinions and of increasing the participation of all members in a discussion so that they can achieve the best possible results. The exercises will also help participants to be more sensitive to the group process which will occur in any discussion in which they may be involved.

18 Stimulating questions

Purpose

It may be that the participants will at some time or other have to act as trainers, extension workers, or do similar tasks. To undertake these functions effectively they will need to know how to combine questions with the discussion based on the methodology they use, i.e. drawing, games, lectures because these methods are only effective if combined with questions and discussion. Therefore before we introduce various types of methodology we should first carry out this exercise with the hope that:

Objectives

1 The participants will be able to explain the meaning of open questions, closed questions and redirected questions.
2 The participants will be able to give examples of the three types of questions mentioned above.
3 The participants will be able to explain the use of each of these types of questions.

Time

120 minutes (2 hours)

Place

A large classroom

Materials

Blackboard and chalk, or large pieces of paper and felt pens

The activity

Introduction
Explain that in all types of situations we ask questions to stimulate discussion and to gain attention. For instance, after a slide show or film appropriate questions can help the group think about the most important issues and ideas raised in the show. There are different types of questions and each has its own use. The three types of questions we will discuss are a) open, b) closed, and c) redirected questions.

Steps
1 Write the three kinds of questions on the paper or blackboard as headings, allowing space under each for sample questions to be written in later.
2 Explain each type of question.
a) Closed questions
A closed question calls for a brief, exact reply. The advantages are that it can focus discussion on a specific point and it can help the trainer or facilitator check whether or not the group understands the content and agrees with the content ideas. Thus, if the participants do not agree - or do not know the correct answer - the trainer can plan additional teaching of the subject. The disadvantage of a closed question is that it may limit discussion by discouraging expression of attitudes related to the topic.

b) Open questions

An open question allows for several different, and often lengthy, answers. The advantage of an open question is that it stimulates thought and provokes people to give opinions. It is a good way to get ideas out in the open for the group to discuss. An open question, however, may not work as an entry point into a discussion with people who are not used to expressing their opinions freely in a group.

c) Redirected questions

A redirected question focuses attention away from the trainer and returns the responsibility of problem solving to the group. When the trainer is asked a question sometimes it is a good idea to ask someone else in the group to answer it. A disadvantage of this technique is that the person to whom the trainer redirects the question may not be prepared to answer it, which makes him or her uncomfortable.

3 Write an example of a closed question under the heading on the board, such as 'When should a mother begin to give porridge to her baby?'

4 Tell the participants to discuss the closed question and to give examples themselves. Write down the advantages and disadvantages of closed questions and when to use them.

5 Write an example of an open question under the heading on the board, such as 'What should a young mother do if her mother-in-law insists on her producing more children?'

6 Ask one of the participants to lead a short discussion on this question. After the discussion ask for other examples of open questions.

7 Write an example of a redirected question on the board, such as 'Mrs. Lis said that her family never drink boiled water and they are never sick. She asks why she should boil water for her baby. This is a good question. Who can answer it?' Continue as in step 6.

Discussion and conclusions

After having some initial problems in differentiating between the types of questions, the participants will probably become interested and compete to give examples of questions.

Exercise adapted, with permission, from *From the Field: Tested Participatory Activities for Trainers*, compiled by Catherine D. Crone and Carman St. John Hunter, New York: World Education, 1980.

19 Dividing sticks

Purpose

In any discussion group there is always someone who speaks a lot and someone who speaks little. To increase the chances of everyone participating more evenly in the discussion this exercise may help. Through this exercise it is hoped that:

Objectives

1 Each participant becomes aware of how much she or he participates in a group discussion.
2 Those participants who tend to dominate a discussion become more prepared to give others a greater opportunity to participate.
3 Those participants who are afraid to express their opinions in the group become more prepared to talk.

Time

This exercise can be undertaken during any group discussion, for example when there is a topic under discussion in groups, or when a two-way lecture/discussion is being held.

Place

Room of sufficient size

Materials

A sufficient number of short sticks (or matches) for each participant to have several. For example, in a group of six people each participant should have about ten sticks.

The activity

Introduction
Explain to the participants that it is preferable if all members of a group take an active part in discussions and that we will now try to give all members of our group a chance to participate actively in the discussion which we are about to have.

Steps
1 Give each participant about ten sticks (or an appropriate number).
2 Tell participants that each time they speak they must place one stick in front of them. When all the sticks are placed in front of them he or she should not speak again.

At the end of the discussion hopefully all members of the group have placed all their sticks out in front.

Discussion and conclusions

The participants are invited to judge to what extent they have participated in the group.

This exercise can be done more than once if it is found to help increase wider participation in discussion groups.

Exercise adapted from A.G. Lunandi, *Laboratorium Sosial*, 1976.

20 Buying and selling a radio

Purpose

One aim of a discussion is to achieve consensus on a problem. To obtain consensus both the result and the process is important because each member of a group will gain greater satisfaction if he or she has had an opportunity to express his or her views. A decision which is reached by just a few members of the group cannot be called consensus (even if the decision may be right). We are all aware of how difficult it is to achieve a satisfactory consensus. Through this exercise it is hoped that:

Objectives

1 The participants can explain the difficulties in achieving consensus in a discussion, and the reasons for these difficulties.
2 The participants gain a greater respect for the opinions and arguments of others in a discussion.

Time

90 minutes

Place

Classroom

Materials

A task which has been prepared in advance, i.e.

- X buys a transistor for $14
- He sells it again for $15
- He then rebuys it for $16
- But he is forced to sell it again for $17

Question: Did X make a gain or a loss? How much?

NOTE: Local currencies can be used for dollars to make the exercise more relevant.

The activity

Introduction

The trainer explains the importance of discussion and the advantages which can be gained from a good discussion.

Steps

1 Write the task on the blackboard and explain it to the participants.
2 Ask the participants to work out the answer individually.
3 Divide the participants into groups of five and ask people to discuss the answers they have worked out, until they reach consensus.

Discussion and conclusions

Points which can be emphasised

1 The results from one group might differ from the results achieved by another group. Also the process will differ. The trainer can discuss with the group why this occurs.
2 The trainer can ask the participants to relate their experiences. What happened and how did they feel during the discussion?

You can note down the principles of a good discussion from the experiences related above. These might include the following:

- the need to listen well during a discussion;

• the need for each member of the group to be given an opportunity to express his or her opinions;
• the importance of recognising the contribution of someone even though he or she finds it difficult to express themselves;
• the opinion of a clever person is not necessarily right, etc.

Answer: X made a profit of $2.00.

Variation

Steps

1 As above.

2 As above.

3 Ask participants what answer they have worked out. Five or six members with differing answers are asked to form a group in the middle of the classroom to discuss their answers until they achieve consensus. The other participants observe the process.

Discussion

As above.

Exercise adapted from A.G. Lunandi, *Laboratorium Sosial*, 1976.

21 The shoe shop

Purpose

The purpose of this exercise is to become aware of how a good group discussion develops. For this reason, this exercise is best used after the participants know each other and the topic of discussion skills has been introduced so that participants know how to carry on an effective discussion and to make decisions effectively. Through this exercise it is hoped that:

Objectives

1 The participants understand how to conduct a good discussion.

2 The participants are aware that it is often counterproductive to force one's opinion on other people.

3 Each participant is prepared to admit that his or her opinion is not always right.

Time

60 minutes

Place

Classroom of sufficient size

Materials

Copies of the case described below for all participants

The activity

Introduction

Often a discussion group fails to achieve any decisions, producing only confusion, misunderstandings and a feeling of dissatisfaction all round.

Steps
1 Divide the participants into groups of five to six people.
2 Select observers to observe each group.
3 Give a copy of the case to each participant.

The case
A buys a pair of shoes for $12. She pays with two $10 notes. Because the shoe shop did not have any small change the two notes were changed for twenty $1 notes at the neighbouring restaurant. A was then given her change. After A had left, the owner of the restaurant came to the shoe shop to tell him that the money he had been given was false. The shoe shop owner gave him two $10 notes in exchange. What was the loss of the shoe shop owner?

NOTE: Again local currencies can be used to make the exercise more relevant.

---

4 Begin group discussion on this problem.

Discussion and conclusions

The trainer can ask the following questions of the observers to start the discussion.
1 Some groups reached a decision quickly but it turned out the decision was wrong. How did this happen?
2 Other groups reached a right decision quickly. How did they discuss the problem?
3 There was also a group which failed to reach a conclusion at all, even though one of the members had the right answer. Why did this happen?

Points which can be emphasised
1 In a discussion group it is necessary for one person to assume leadership of the group to regulate the discussion.
2 Every opinion should be heard, and then its logic be tested. Not all opinions are necessarily correct.
3 Skills are needed to be able to express one's opinion so that it is clearly understood by others.
4 All members of the group should be convinced of the final conclusions of the group.
Answer: The owner of the shoe shop made a loss of $20.

Exercise adapted from A.G. Lunandi, *Laboratorium Sosial*, 1976.

7 Working together: team work skills

A basic belief underlying community health and community development programmes is that all people have the potential to contribute to their own development and that of their community. This belief has far reaching consequences for programme strategy. It is a basic reason for placing community participation as the cornerstone of community health programmes. It also implies the foregone conclusion that all community workers will constantly be involved in situations requiring them to cooperate with other people. It may be with individuals - the village head, a midwife, farmer or religious leader, or with groups - both formal and informal, or with co-workers.

Cooperation demands working together with a common goal, a concern for each other, and a common understanding of each other's role. To achieve this it is important for all community workers to have an understanding of the dynamics of working together effectively and the skills necessary to achieve this end.

The training situation, where people from different backgrounds are together all day every day for a certain period, offers an excellent opportunity to increase people's skills in working with others and in groups as teams. If exercises which highlight the advantages and problems of working together and techniques for promoting cooperation are given as early as possible in the training, continuing reference can be made to the trainees capacity to cooperate. In order to increase the trainees' awareness of the importance of working together and of developing the necessary skills, the trainers should create a variety of situations in which trainees need to complete tasks in groups and as teams. This could be in the class situation through discussion or task groups, in the field during visits, or through committees to organise, for example, recreational activities or accommodation. When analysing any group task on its completion, reference should also be made to the group process, including the ability of the group members to work together smoothly and productively.

22 Working together, drawing together

Purpose

Activities aimed at improved community life will be most successful if all parties can work together. The same is true of the participants during the training. If there is not good cooperation between the participants, the training will not achieve maximum potential. Therefore, *it is recommended that this game* (or Broken Squares [see Exercise 23], or a similar game) *be included at an early stage of the training programme.*

Objectives

1 The participants can explain those factors which hinder and those which promote good cooperation.
2 The participants become aware of the importance and advantages of working together.

Time

75-90 minutes

Place

Wide enough for several tables

Materials

One piece of paper about 30 × 30 cm for each participant. Several coloured felt pens for each group

The activity

Introduction
Ask the participants the difference between several people doing the same task separately and doing the same task together. Summarise the difference. Mention several advantages of working together.

Steps

1 Divide the participants into groups of four to six. Each group should sit around a table.

2 Give each person in the group a piece of paper (30 × 30 cm), and give the group several felt pens of different colours. Instruct the participants to begin drawing on their piece of paper a subject of their own choice.

3 After two to three minutes, ask the participants to stop drawing and pass their piece of paper onto the next person. Each person should then continue with the incomplete drawing they received.

4 After another two to three minutes, repeat the process.

5 Repeat until each person has their own drawing. If the group has only four members, pass the paper around twice.

6 Give each participant time to look at his or her picture.

Discussion and conclusions

Observing the participants while they are drawing will help the discussion as the trainer can direct questions to the most appropriate people.

Points which can be emphasised

1 When you added to someone else's drawing, did you understand what that person was trying to draw?

2 Were the additions to your picture appropriate and relevant? Is your picture better or worse than you had hoped? Why?

3 How did you feel if the picture you wanted to draw was changed? Why did you feel that way?

4 What did you do if the picture you received was almost complete? How did you feel?

5 How did you feel if the picture you received had just been started?

6 Was anyone afraid to add to a picture? Why?

7 Did anyone find it difficult to add to a picture? Why? Did anyo it easy to add to a picture? Why?

The several conclusions which have been reached about cooperation (see Broken Squares for a more complete explanation) can be listed on the board or large papers.

Exercise adapted from A.G. Lunandi, *Laboratorium Sosial*, 1976.

23 Broken squares

Purpose

Every activity within a community based health programme can only be successful if all parties are prepared to cooperate. The same applies to the trainees. If cooperation between the trainees is lacking, the training will have limited success. The 'Broken Squares' game might thus be presented at the beginning of the training course with the hope that:

Objectives

1 Participants can explain those factors which both hinder and encourage good teamwork.
2 Participants are conscious of the importance of making an effort to cooperate with each other.

Time

60-75 minutes

Place

Sufficient space for several tables, or sufficient floor space

Materials

Five envelopes (A,B,C,D,E) each of which contains pieces of the five squares as follows:

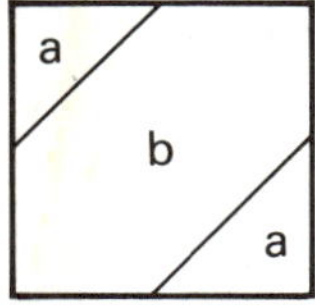

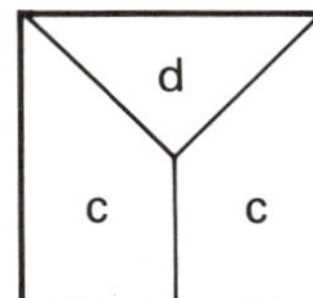

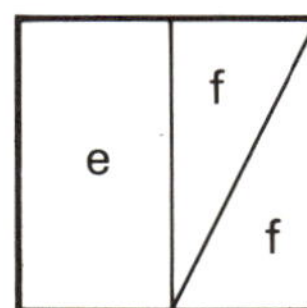

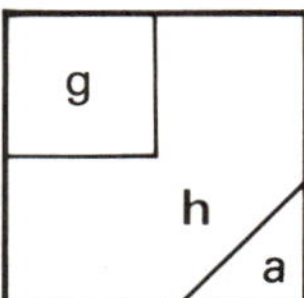

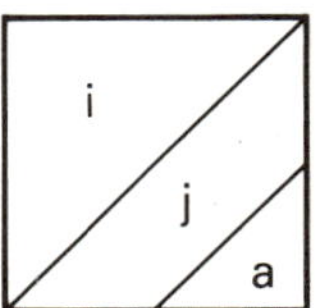

The squares should be made of cardboard of sufficient thickness.

- Envelope A contains pieces i,h,e
- Envelope B contains pieces a,a,a,c
- Envelope C contains pieces a,j
- Envelope D contains pieces d,f
- Envelope E contains b,c,f,g

A table for each team

The activity

Introduction
Briefly explain the difference between working together and teamwork. Mention some of the advantages of teamwork. Then explain that each

group of five will be given a set of envelopes which contain the pieces of five squares. (If necessary explain the meaning of square).

Steps

1 Prepare the material:

- instructions for players (see page 60);
- instructions for observers (see page 60);
- pieces of the squares (see page 57 for directions on how to make them).

2 Divide the participants into small groups, containing five players and one or two observers, according to the number of participants. Each group forms a separate circle.

3 Before beginning, give out the instructions to the players and the observers, and explain them.

4 Explain that each group will be issued with five envelopes containing pieces of a square. None of the envelopes contain pieces for a complete square.

5 When everyone has understood the directions, begin. During the game the trainer observes the groups in order to gather information on individual reactions to be used later in the discussion.

Discussion and conclusions

Before beginning the discussion it should be explained that the results of the observations are not a personal attack but an opportunity to learn. The discussion can then proceed as follows:

1 Listen to the reports of the observers.

2 Discuss the feelings of the players.

3 Ask the players to give their opinions.

Points which can be emphasised

4 Several relevant questions that can be asked.

- How did you feel when you had to receive all the pieces?
- How did you feel when you saw that a companion could not finish his task?
- How did you view a companion that was self absorbed and did not want to give a required piece?
- How did you feel when you were not holding a piece?
- How did you feel when you were given a piece that you did not require? or that you did require?
- How did you feel when you could not complete your square?
- How did you feel when you had successfully completed your square?

5 You can use the cases which arise from observations and disclosures by the players. You can draw from them points which are relevant to the functions and tasks of the trainees.

a) Case: One participant gave all the pieces to a colleague.
Conclusion: Teamwork is hindered if someone rejects responsibility and places it all on someone else.

b) Case: One participant collected all the pieces and refused to part with them.
Conclusion: Teamwork is hampered when one member receives everything and wants to work hard to complete it himself.

c) Case: A participant is self-satisfied after finishing his or her square, and ignores the other participants.
Conclusion: Teamwork is hampered if one member is satisfied with his own effort and does not care about the work of the other members.

d) Case: A participant was frustrated when he or she knew the correct piece was held by a colleague who would not relinquish it.
Conclusion: Teamwork is hampered if one member is insensitive to the needs of others.

e) Case: A participant was very pleased to receive a piece which he or she wanted from a colleague.
Conclusion: Teamwork is promoted by a sensitive member responding to a need.

f) Case: A participant broke the rules and communicated with a colleague (by word or sign) because he or she wanted to help.
Conclusion: In teamwork there must be mutual communication between members.

And still other cases will arise from which conclusions can be drawn.

The following principles of teamwork can then be deduced from the previous discussion.

1 Team members must give in accordance to the need of other team members. This means:

- being sensitive to what is required;
- being open in one's relationship with others;
- recognising and admitting the difficulties, wanting to assist other people.

2 Team members must be conscious of, and prepared to recognise the abilities of other colleagues.

3 Each person must be able to understand how he or she can help towards solving a problem.

4 Each person must understand the problem.

5 There must be mutual communication between the team members.

6 There must be coordination among team members.

Exercise adapted, with permission, from *From the Field: Tested Participatory Activities for Trainers*, compiled by Catherine D. Crone and Carman St. John Hunter, New York: World Education, 1980.

Instructions for players

1 Each member of the group has to make one square (four sides must be of equal length).

2 The game will be considered finished when each participant has a completed square in front of him.

3 Each square is the same size.

4 No one must speak while the game is in progress.

5 It is forbidden to ask for a piece, either directly or by sign.

6 It is not permitted to take a piece from a colleague.

7 It is not permitted to assist a colleague make his square.

8 A piece may be given to a colleague, who *must* receive it.

9 When a piece is given, it must be clear who it is given to, it must not just be put in the middle.

10 A completed square may be given to a colleague if desired.

11 Begin working when the order is given.

Instructions for observers

Observe closely, note down and report what happens in the group while the game is in progress.

1 Did any member of the group disobey the rules?
What rule was broken? Why do you think it was broken?

2 Did any member like to give pieces to colleagues?

3 Did any member disregard the efforts and difficulties of his colleagues after his own square was completed?

4 Did anyone become upset, confused or lose hope because of difficulty in forming the square?

5 Did any member collect pieces and become unwilling to relinquish them to other colleagues?

6 Was any member unable to participate because he or she did not have any pieces?

24 Group drawing

Purpose

If a group or organisation is to do the best work possible for their common tasks, each individual member must clearly understand the real aim of the group and of the task to be performed. By means of this exercise it is hoped that:

Objectives

1 Participants will realise the importance of a clear formulation of the aim of the group before starting an activity.
2 Participants will realise the importance of inter-communication between members of the group.

Time

45-60 minutes

Place

Enough space for participants, in groups of four or five persons, to be able to draw

Materials

One large piece of paper per group
Coloured felt pens, one colour for each person
Thumb tacks, pens or tape for fastening the paper

The activity

Introduction
Explain that the purpose is to draw a picture of the group in which the participant is working in which the group is described in terms of its composition, aspirations, etc.

Steps
1 Divide participants into groups of four to five people.
2 Distribute paper and felt pens.
3 Ask participants to begin drawing a picture that symbolises their group without communicating with any other member.

4 Tell the group that each member is free to add anything which he or she considers necessary to perfect the group picture.
5 When finished, ask the group to fasten the picture on the wall.

Discussion and conclusions

Each group explains their picture, including the process of its formation, despite the lack of communication and agreement. The discussion should focus on the teamwork: whether each one took part or whether one member dominated, etc.

Points which can be emphasised
From the results of the discussion of each group, the principles of teamwork can be emphasised:
- each member should contribute;
- there must be two-way communication etc.

(See the conclusion of 'Broken Squares', Exercise 23, for more complete discussion.)

25 Win the most

Purpose

It is easy to talk of the necessity of teamwork among many groups in order to achieve a specific aim but it is hard to put it into practice. In real life, the basic motive in teamwork is often not 'what is the best for everyone' but 'what is best for my group'. If that is the viewpoint of community groups, 'teamwork' can fall to pieces. Through 'Win the Most' it is hoped:

Objectives

1 Participants will realise the importance of considering the interests of all parties.
2 In considering the interests of others, the participants will be able to work more effectively as a team.

Time

90 minutes

Place

A classroom of sufficient size

Materials

Four cards marked 'A' and four marked 'B', each measuring 10 × 10 cm
'Win the Most' scoring form for each group (see following Card A)
The form containing the text 'Winning and Losing Situations' for each group (Card B)
A small table in the middle of the room for opening the chosen card

The activity

Introduction
Introduce the game to the participants and give instructions for playing it. Suggest that each group does its very best to win.

Steps
1 Divide the participants into four groups, one in each corner of the classroom. Each group should be some distance away from any other group. The size of each group will depend on the number of participants.

2 Give each group two cards, A and B.

3 Give the 'Win the Most' instruction sheet to each participant, and explain its contents if necessary.

4 Supervise the game and divide the time from round 1 to round 10, according to the 'Win the Most' instruction sheet.

5 Make notes of every aspect (comments, reactions, cheating etc.) for discussion.

6 After the tenth round, each participant returns to his or her place, and counts his or her score.

Card A

Directions

In 10 consecutive rounds each group will choose one of two letters, A or B. Your group's score will depend on the pattern of choice of the four participating groups, as follows:

4A =	each	Lose	200	2B =	each	Lose	200
3A =	each	Win	100	1A =		Win	300
1B =		Lose	300	3B =	each	Lose	100
2A =	each	Win	200	4B =	each	Lose	100

Rules

Before deciding on your group's choice consult your colleagues in order to have a unanimous decision. After the time is up and each group has made its choice, a representative is sent to the small table with the card chosen by the group (keeping its contents secret). On a signal from the trainer all four cards are placed number up on the table. You may consult the other three groups only before rounds 5, 8 and 10 to decide on your choice. Each group can send a representative to negotiate with any other group. The representative then tells his group the results. Each group then makes its choice.

Round	*Time*	*Consultation*	*Choice*	*Win*	*Lose*	*Balance*
1	2 min	Within group				
2	1 min	"				
3	1 min	"				
4	1 min	"				
5	3 min	Other groups				×3
	1 min	Within group				
6	1 min	"				
7	1 min	"				
8	3 min	Other groups				×5
	1 min	Within group				
9	1 min	"				
10	3 min	Other groups				×10
	1 min	Within group				

The trainer should give an opportunity to all participants to pour out their feelings.

Discussion and conclusions

Points which can be emphasised

These questions might be asked:

1 How does it feel to be a person/group that has been cheated?
2 How does the group that cheated another group feel?
3 Do the members of the winning group feel really satisfied?
4 Why were the rules not observed by all groups in the same way?
5 What can we learn from this game if we relate it to everyday happenings?

As a conclusion to the game, give out the sheet 'Winning and Losing Situations' and read it out aloud or invite each participant to read it. It has been frequently seen that, after reading this, the participants will draw a deep breath and will mutter to themselves, laughing softly, indicating their realisation that it is not good to win alone.

Card B

Winning and losing situations

Where importance is placed on winning, it is possible that there will be competitiveness even when it is not warranted. Think of how many meetings we have experienced in which the purpose is to make the very best decision concerning a certain activity, but which suddenly become a battlefield. The participants no longer listen to their colleagues' data, because they are too busy thinking of how they can present their own opinions, or challenge other people's suggestions in order to win.

We also know that what is called dialogue between two colleagues, or two groups, or between social forces and the government, is in fact often only a struggle to win. How often victories in this 'win or lose struggle' turn into defeat for both sides. We can say that it is a double loss.

Below several results are listed that can arise from a 'win or lose' situation. The list follows no particular order, nor is it complete:

1 Wastes time and energy outside the main discussion.
2 Hinders decision-making.
3 Causes deadlocks.
4 Isolates participants who do not like trouble.
5 Makes it difficult to listen.
6 Hinders the exploration of possibilities.
7 Lessens, sometimes destroys, sensitivity.
8 Leads to the loss of participants.
9 Arouses destructive anger.
10 Loses sympathy.
11 Gives rise to a tendency to dissatisfaction.
12 Causes enmity.
13 Provokes personal attacks.
14 Causes the erection of barriers of self defence.

We can be certain that at some time we will be confronted by 'win or lose' situations, and therefore it is important for us to be able to see if a situation is becoming threatening. In a two party conflict, you can be the one who stops attacking your colleague. He or she will not be able to go on fighting by him or herself. Try to give priority to what is best for all parties, rather than be blinded by the desire to win.

8 *Moving together: leadership skills*

The underlying goal of all community health and community development work is human development. It is the goal of training activities too. In both situations the development of leadership qualities are included. Every community worker will find him or herself in leadership roles in a variety of situations - facilitating a meeting, speaking with a women's group, or discussing plans with a group of volunteer health workers. There will also be times when they need to play an active role in promoting and increasing the participation of people and groups. They will also be working together with both formal and informal leaders with different leadership styles.

In approaching such situations queries will no doubt arise in their minds: How should I tackle this situation? What is the best leadership style for me to assume? How can I weld the group together? and many others. It is clear from these questions that leadership skills cover a wide range. For example, communicating and teamwork building skills are two that are essential. However, it is also valuable to have an understanding of leadership styles and techniques which are studied through the exercises in this section.

After discussing various aspects of leadership and attempting to put them into practice during the training, it is hoped that the trainees will have increased their aptitude and their skills as leaders.

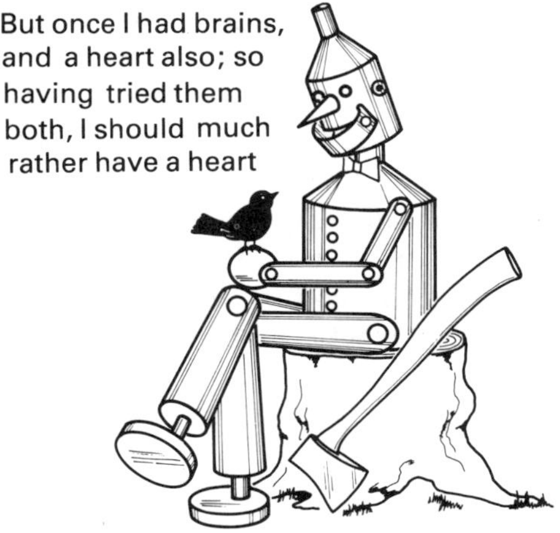

26 Guiding discussion

Purpose

After the problem of leadership has been discussed, the trainer may like to give the participants an opportunity to practice as leaders. This leadership role play is easy to present before a meeting. Through this exercise it is hoped that:

Objectives

1 Participants understand the importance of the proper atmosphere for a good group discussion.
2 Participants realise the importance of the role of the leader of a discussion in determining the framework and the systematic development of the discussion.
3 The trainees are able to observe and take action in relation to the interaction of the participants of the discussion.
4 The participants understand the function of a leader in relation to a discussion.
5 Participants understand the requirements of a good discussion.

Time

90-120 minutes

Place

A room large enough not to confine the discussion group and the observer

Materials

Blackboard and chalk

A description of the situation in 'Example' or some other topic, given to everyone

Instructions for the five players
Name cards for the five players
A table and chairs for the players
Directions for observers

The activity

Introduction
The trainer explains the requirements of a good discussion.

Steps
1 Choose five players (best to choose people who have no difficulty speaking).
2 Explain the problem to be discussed, then give each of the players instructions for the role they will be presenting.
3 Ask the other participants to observe. Explain that from this exercise various aspects of leadership will be discussed. The observers should look at the meeting in its entirety, including:

- the role and leadership functions of the 'leader';
- the attitude and reactions of the 'led'.

NOTE: the players must not be aware of the directions given to the observers.

4 Check to see that everyone understands his or her task. Where there are two trainers, one assists the players, while the other assists the group of observers.
5 When everything is ready, the exercise may proceed. The players should arrange their own chairs.
6 Stop the exercise when you think there is enough material for discussion.

Discussion and conclusions

Points which can be emphasised
1 Seating arrangement - circular or not?
• The seating arrangement and an atmosphere of sharing and mutual respect are extremely important in determining the results and the process of discussion. This is the task of the leader.
• A circular seating arrangement is good, as everyone can see each other and it reinforces equality.
2 How did the leader present the problem?
• Did he or she outline the problem for the members? In a discussion it is extremely important that each member understands the broad outline of the problem under discussion. In this way it is hoped that they will feel the need to solve the problem together.
• Did the leader present the matter as his or her own idea? This is less attractive because it emphasises his or her own importance. Interest will be heightened if the idea is submitted as the idea of the group. In fact it would be more interesting to ask someone else to put forward the idea, and someone else to enlarge upon it. So from the very beginning the idea belongs to the group.
3 How does the leader react to the opinion of the members?
• Discussion does not consist of questions and answers between leader and the members; it should be a matter of mutual give and take. Remember that the task of the leader is to provide an opportunity for all the members to freely propose and accept each others' opinions.

• The leader should ask another member for his response to someone else's opinion. In this way a dialogue will develop.

4 Who will summarise the discussion?

• This should not always be done by the leader, as it will certainly be in accordance with his or her own interests. Ask another member to summarise the results of the discussion, and ask other members for their response. In this way the meeting will be alive, and the conclusion more objective.

• The leader tightens up the conclusions from the members.

5 Was there movement, or a change of expression among the participants of the meeting?

• As the leader, or participants of a meeting, we must not only pay attention to what is said, but to the entire atmosphere, as words are not the only form of expression.

6 Was there an attempt to explain things to each other?

• As leader, it is good to occasionally clarify the opinion of a participant.

• The leader may also check the opinion of a participant with another participant. In this way errors of interpretation will be lessened.

• By these means smooth communication is ensured during the meeting; participants will not be sleepy, and will all feel involved.

7 What was the attitude of the leader to conflict within the meeting?

• It is unprofitable for the leader to take sides or give direct support to one side in a conflict situation.

• The leader should propose questions, or ask the opinion of other participants. In this way the antagonists will be made to realise the situation.

• To pressure a participant who rejects or does not agree with the view or the idea of another participant only adds to the negative reaction of those involved. Personal requirements must be heard. This is most necessary for setting criteria for the evaluation of various views.

A leader is good, if within the group he or she:

• is prepared to apportion functions, and does not keep all for himself or herself;
• works so that members assume leadership functions;
• takes over only those functions that have not been taken by other members;
• understands and is able to assume all functions if necessary.

Problems that may arise

The players may not carry out instructions properly, with the result that there is not enough material for discussion.

Example of problems to be presented in role playing

This is one example of a role play. This example may be used if it reflects a local situation; otherwise compose a more appropriate one.

Whatever problem is used it must contain these elements:

• a difference of interests between the participants of the meeting;

- a difference of opinion between the participants about the subject under discussion;
- the wish by the leader for a quick decision.

Example
Although several families have begun to construct toilets for themselves, the village wants to build public toilets, because this has been done elsewhere. However, there are other projects which are also considered necessary and are thought by some to have a higher priority.

Instructions
Village Head: wants a decision about the public toilets to be made quickly.
Teacher: does not fully agree, but wants to know more about the public toilets, so that the programme will be better prepared.
Neighbourhood leader: agrees, as long as the toilet is in his locality. If not, he will not help.
Neighbourhood leader: is indifferent, because he is busy with his own personal concerns.
Leading personality in the community: agrees, because he wants to topple the teacher.

NOTE: The type of project/example may be altered in accordance with the local situation.

Directions for observers

This exercise provides an opportunity to analyse several matters related to the function of a leader in opening and conducting a discussion. Try to observe the meeting as a whole, as well as trying to answer questions such as the following:
1 Was there an attempt, in the opening, to create an atmosphere of comradeship?
2 Was the seating arrangement good, so that everyone could see each other?
3 How was the subject presented?
a) Was it presented so that it seemed to be a group problem?
b) Was it presented as if it was the leader's problem?
c) Was it presented so that every member could give his opinion?
4 How did the participants react to the topic that was presented?
5 What was the reaction of the leader to the reaction of the other members?
a) Did he accept all their ideas?
b) Did he give members an opportunity to reply to the ideas of other members?
c) Did the leader explain every idea or comment on it?

Observe the attitude, the manner, and the words of each participant, and the reaction of the other participants.

27 Clean the mirror

Purpose

The person who has been given the responsibility of leadership must form good relations with his or her group. This is a relationship in which it will always be possible for each party to develop. Each person that takes part in a community programme should also take over some leadership functions. He or she therefore can be assisted if there is an opportunity to observe factors which promote leadership. Through this exercise of mirror cleaning it is hoped:

Objectives

1 Participants will be better able to understand and carry out some of the functions and work of a leader.
2 Participants will appreciate some of the functions and tasks of people who take on leadership roles.

Time

30-45 minutes

Place

A room of sufficient size

Materials

None

The activity

Introduction

Steps
1 Choose ten or more of the participants.
2 Ask the participants to form two lines facing each other (five people on the left and five on the right), and pretend that there is a big mirror between them.
3 Explain that the participants on the right will be asked to clean the mirror in front of them.

4 The participants in front of them will act as their reflection and copy every movement for about three minutes.
5 Give the instruction to begin.
6 After three minutes reverse the roles so that the cleaner becomes the reflection and vice versa.

NOTE: This exercise is done all together.

Discussion and conclusions

1 You can take as a starting point for discussion the observation, experience and impressions of the participants.
2 You can describe the work, the function and the behaviour of a good leader, bearing in mind that a leader has people under him, or people who he leads.

You can direct the discussion with questions such as those which follow:

- Did you attempt to simplify your movements when you were cleaning the mirror? What was your reason for not doing so? If you simplified them, what was your reason?
- Did you try as hard as you could to copy the movements when you were the reflection?
- Did you find it hard to be the reflection? Why?
- How did you feel if you saw your reflection copy your movements incorrectly? Did you reprimand him or her?
- Which was the easiest - to be the cleaner or the reflection?
- Did you realise that while you were cleaning the mirror you had become the leader?
- While you were cleaning the mirror did you think of your reflection?

Points which can be emphasised
1 A leader should always consider the ability of those under him or her.
2 A lack of self awareness on the part of the leader will have a big effect on those under him or her.
3 A leader must be able to provide a good example.
4 It is hard to be a leader, but it is even more difficult to be one of the followers.
5 The relationship between a leader and those under him or her is *not* the same as the relationship between a mirror and its reflection.

28 On the moon

Purpose

Purpose

Peoples' participation is critical to every aspect of development - especially development of village communities. Participation is achieved through a certain pattern of approach. However, if we were to make an appraisal, we would find a big tendency towards the top down/dictator approach (from the top to the bottom). Through this exercise it is hoped that:

Objectives

1 Participants can make a comparison of the advantages and disadvantages of the dictator approach, and an approach from below.
2 Participants can see why the approach from below is more advantageous that the dictator approach from above.

Time

40-60 minutes

Place

A classroom of sufficient size

Materials

Three handkerchiefs large enough to bandage the eyes
Three chairs for 'earth stations'
Objects (representing planets and stars) that can serve as obstacles for the astronauts' journey to the moon (e.g. chair, book, stone or other objects near at hand)
Three flags for each of the astronauts to plant on the moon
Three chairs representing the moon

The activity

Introduction
The trainer explains that there are two types of approaches:'
- the dictator approach, top down;
- the approach from below, bottom up.

Steps
1 Ask six volunteers from among the participants to come to the front.
2 Divide the six into three groups of two people.
3 Ask each pair to decide on their roles: one will be the astronaut and the other will be the earth station.
4 Ask some other participants to arrange the area: chairs for the earth stations to sit; obstacles (such as stars, planets which are scattered about) and a moon for each astronaut.
5 Cover the eyes of the astronauts with a handkerchief.
6 State the task of the earth stations, the astronauts, and the observers.
Task of the earth stations: to give orders/commands to the astronaut whose eyes are covered, so he or she can reach the moon to plant his or her flag without touching any obstacles.
Task of the astronauts: to follow the commands of the earth station in order to reach the moon and plant the flag without touching any of the obstacles.
Task of the other participants: to observe the progress of the game.

Each time an astronaut touches an obstacle, he must return to earth and start again. After 30 minutes, stop the exercise whether or not an astronaut has reached the moon.

Discussion and conclusions

To focus the discussion:

1 The trainer can ask each astronaut how he or she felt while they were getting orders from the earth station without being allowed to react.

2 The trainer can ask each earth station how he or she felt while giving orders and being responsible for the safety of the astronauts.

3 The trainer can ask for responses/comments from the observers.

During discussion, the following comments are sure to arise.

- The astronaut hesitated to take a step because he did not feel confident enough of the orders of the earth station.
- The astronauts were disturbed by the voices of the earth stations, so that they often made mistakes (too many commands and not enough coordination).
- The astronauts felt frustrated because they were not allowed to make their own moves (their eyes were covered).

Points which can be emphasised

1 There will be better participation in an activity if, among other things:

- participants are invited to take part in the planning and the implementation;
- there is mutual trust between the leader and the others;
- participants feel they will gain some benefit.

2 A programme which is implemented by several parties will be more successful if it is coordinated.

3 It is better, in attempting community development, to use an approach from below, with nurturing and help from above, rather than use the dictator approach.

29 Guiding the blind

Purpose

In community work, much of our energy is channelled to provide assistance and guidance. In such circumstances it is to be hoped that participants will have attitudes which are necessary for such work to be a success. Through this exercise it is hoped that:

Objectives

1 Participants can understand the feeling of the 'blind' in the sense of 'not knowing' and 'not understanding'.
2 Participants are more sensitive to the feelings and the needs of those they are helping.
3 Participants understand some of the conditions for guidance and nurturing.

Time

60 minutes

Place

In and about the classroom

Materials

A piece of material or handkerchief of a dark colour

The activity

Introduction
Explain that someone who has the job of nurturing and guiding should have certain attitudes in order to do the work well.

Steps
1 Divide the participants into two groups, A and B. Everyone in group A is blindfolded with a piece of material or a large dark handkerchief, so that they cannot see at all.

2 Everyone in B group (not blindfolded) chooses someone from group A as their partner, and for 10–15 minutes guides them in an activity so they have the feeling of using their other senses.
3 Remove blindfolds from group A and return to places for discussion.

Discussion and conclusions

The trainer can ask questions such as the following:
Questions to Group A (those who were guided)
1 How did you feel while you were blindfolded?
2 What was your greatest impression while you were blindfolded?
3 What was your feeling about the person who was guiding you?
- Were you suspicious? Why?
- Did you feel you had his or her attention?
- Did you feel that you were being laughed at?

Questions to Group B (those who guided)
1 How did you feel while you were guiding someone?
2 What things did you purposefully do while you were guiding him or her?
- Look for easy things for him or her to do?
- Look for difficult things?
- Give your entire attention to him or her?
- Sometimes leave him or her to his or her own free movement?
- Did you talk about the situation confronting you?

From the answers and comments of the players, we can come to several conclusions, about the best attitude for someone to have, the best steps to take, and the best things to do, when giving care and guidance.

Points which can be emphasised
A good guide/supervisor:
1 does not leave those he is guiding to do as they like;
2 but also does not bind them so that they may do only what he wants;
3 always offers natural explanations, does not try to make them afraid or to belittle the obstacles that they face;
4 bases action upon the feelings and the ability of those being guided;
5 surrenders to those being guided, the tasks which they are able to do.

Adapted, with permission, from *From the Field: Tested Participatory Activities for Trainers*, compiled by Catherine D. Crone and Carman St. John Hunter, New York: World Education, 1980.

9 Planning together: community development skills

Health workers and those from other fields who are beginning work with communities will soon realise that they are expected to be extra resourceful as they have little or no immediate back-up support once they leave the walls of their office or institution. To work with the heterogenous members of a community they will need to be sensitive, creative, open, flexible, and willing to listen and to persevere even though they may face setbacks and disappointments.

Apart from these attitudes they will also need knowledge and skills to assist a community in making adequate preparations and to sit together with key people to plan activities aimed at increasing the health and well-being of the community. In other words, community work demands knowledge, skills and attitudes which are additional to those needed in a clinic or office setting.

During training it is possible to increase trainees' awareness of the importance of certain attitudes and skills and to challenge them to begin to develop some of these skills. In this final section we present exercises which will help to sensitise the trainees to the signifcance of being flexible and creative. These exercises also focus on the importance of sensitivity in determining the felt needs of a community. The final set of exercises are concrete planning exercises. They allow participants to

examine their new knowledge in applying it to the basic community health/development techniques of social preparation and participative planning.

These topics will be most effectively covered after discussions on communication, teamwork and leadership.

Planning

After training each participant is expected to use what he or she has learned, according to his or her particular function. All work and every activity that is to be carried out must be well planned. Good planning will facilitate the achievement of the required aim. Because of this, in every training planning must be discussed and studied intensively. So that the discussion on planning will influence the work that will eventually be done by the participants, at the end of the training they should draw up a plan of action to be carried out on their return home from the training. Before the plan is made discuss techniques of good planning.

30 Consolidating understanding of social preparation[1]

Purpose

Often communities are resistant to new ideas and therefore they do not readily accept and implement them. To help overcome this problem it is necessary for the participants to realise the great importance of social preparation. To enable participants to more fully absorb the application of social preparation they are presented with actual cases. By means of this exercise it is hoped that:

Objectives

1 Participants realise the importance of social preparation.
2 Participants realise the importance of all parties involved in a programme taking part from the beginning.
3 Participants will be able to explain the steps to be taken in the process of preparing a community or community groups.

Time

60-90 minutes

Place

An area with sufficient space for group discussion

Materials

A piece of paper on which the case is written together with answers (five appropriate steps in the order in which they are to be taken, and five inappropriate steps). *This is for the trainer only.*

Three to four sets of the exercise, each set consisting of eleven pieces of thick paper (e.g. manilla paper) approx. 20 × 8 cm. Each piece has one step written on it, but no numbers. The eleventh piece has the case written on it.

1 Social preparation is the process by which planners work with community people to develop both the process and strategy on which a community based health programme can be developed. See Appendix I for the full description.

The activity

Introduction
Explain the instructions and the relevance of the exercise to the topic of Social Preparation.

Steps
1 Divide participants into groups of approximately six people.
2 Each group discusses the given case and tries to determine what steps should be taken.
3 The group then studies the ten steps which are provided and tries to choose the five most appropriate steps (in line with their discussion) and arrange them in the most appropriate order.
4 After deciding on the appropriate order, each group presents their conclusions and the reasons for the order.
5 The trainer can discuss differences in group findings and the key given in the exercise, if any. Reasons for differences can be explored.

Discussion and conclusions

When each group has arranged the five steps in the order which they consider to be the most appropriate you can ask the groups to explain their reasons and then give other groups the opportunity to ask about or comment on anything that is still not clear.

Example: A guide for the trainer

Case
The clinic team has decided to try to set up a community health programme aimed at improving the health of children in several of the villages surrounding the rural clinic. The objective is to encourage the villagers to become active in preventive programmes in order to both improve health status and reduce the clinic load.

Most appropriate steps in the order in which they might be carried out

1 Introduce yourselves to the village head.

2 With the village head, contact community leaders and together compile information on existing problems gathered from the community, the government service, and local organisations.

3 Discuss and analyse the problems to determine which can be handled first.

4 With community leaders look for more concrete information from other government services and organisations.

5 Attend a meeting with the village head which is also attended by community leaders and the community in general, at which the team provides practical information.

Least appropriate steps

1 Give mothers a list of tasks which they must carry out to keep their children healthy.

2 Order the people, through the village head, to bring all sick children to the clinic for treatment.

3 Ask an appropriate agency to provide 'Road to Health' charts for all mothers with children under five so that mothers can be made aware of the connection between weight loss and poor health.

4 Order the village to begin a programme to train mothers to weigh their babies and to take babies who fail to grow to the clinic.

5 Order the people, through the village head, to bring all children to a central place to assess their disease problems.

NOTE: You can easily use a scenario more appropriate to local situations or adapt this one to your own conditions.

---

31 Guessing what is needed

Purpose

When the subject of Social Preparation is being discussed with the participants, they should realise that it is not easy to know the exact needs of other people or the needs felt by a community. Through this exercise it is hoped that:

Objectives

1 Participants realise that we often consider the needs of others from the viewpoint of our own interests.

2 Participants understand those factors which enhance their efforts to gain a more precise understanding of the needs of others.

Time

30-45 minutes

Place

Classroom

Materials

Paper for each participant to make notes

The activity

Introduction
One necessary step in preparing a community is to know the community's needs. But this is not an easy task.

Steps
1 Divide participants into pairs.
2 Ask each participant to write three needs which he or she thinks are felt at the time by his or her partner, and three of his or her own needs. Partners may not speak to each other. (Five minutes is sufficient time.)
3 In turn one of the pairs reads out the needs of his or her partner and then his or her own needs. Then his or her partner reads out his or her own needs, and his or her partners' needs. Ask three or four pairs to read out their needs like this.

The trainer asks:

- Were your guesses of your partner's needs correct?
- Were your guesses different from the needs he or she felt?
- How did the difference arise?
- Why are some guesses right?

Discussion and conclusions

Points which can be emphasised
1 There is a possibility that we sometimes fail to see the requirements of others in the same way that they see and feel them.
2 There is a tendency to think that others have the same needs as we feel ourselves.

3 It can greatly help to know the needs of others if communication with them.
4 Because of this fact we need to have direct communic community in order to discover the precise needs that the

Exercise adapted, with permission, from *From the Participatory Activities for Trainers*, compiled by Catherine D. Crone and Carman St. John Hunter, New York: World Education, 1980.

32 Making the longest line

Purpose

Every person, and every group of people, possess ability. It is important that every community worker is prepared to see and to recognise that ability, and develop skills which help the community members realise their own potential. In addition, he or she must be able to encourage community people willing to use all the potential they have.

Objectives

1 Participants realise that anyone, anywhere, and at all times, has abilities.
2 Participants understand that by using all the abilities available an activity is almost certain to be more successful.
3 Participants will be more creative.

Time

30 minutes

Place

A place of sufficient size

Materials

None

The activity

Introduction
Even though we do not always realise it, every person and every group of persons possess abilities. We want to try to prove it.

Steps
1 Ask participants to form two groups.
2 Instruct each group to make a line as long as possible across the room using anything they have on their persons. They must not get anything from anywhere else. They are to be told that they have ten minutes to complete the task.
3 At the end of ten minutes the trainer judges the longest line.

Discussion and conclusions

The trainer can ask the following questions:
1 Which group made the longest line?
2 What factors made that group win?
3 What steps did that group take to win?, e.g. in order to make the longest line, someone may lie down, use a belt, etc.

Points which can be emphasised

1 A great deal of creativity is demanded to discover and put abilities to their maximum use.

2 The abilities of everyone can be used, as long as whoever has the ability is willing to participate.

3 A community worker must understand how to motivate the community so that they use the abilities that they have.

33 Filling in circles

Purpose

Being active in community programmes, we come across many social problems. Sometimes the problem demands a solution in a relatively short time. For this we need to think quickly and creatively. Through the exercise below it is hoped:

Objectives

Participants can increase their creativity and speed of thinking.

Time

20 minutes

Place

Room of sufficient size

Materials

A form covered with circles for each participant (see facing page)
A large piece of paper and a coloured felt pen, or blackboard and chalk

The activity

Introduction

Explain that one of the demands made on a community worker is to solve a problem in a short time.

Steps

1 Hand the folded forms out to the participants.

Participants may not touch the forms until instructed to do so.

2 Give the sign to begin. The participants must fill the circles with the name of any round objects, e.g. ball, as quickly as possible.

3 After approximately ten minutes give the sign to stop.

Discussion and conclusions

The trainer asks:

- Who filled less than 5 circles? Why?
- Who was able to fill 6-10? Why?
- Who was able to fill 11-15? Why?
- Who filled 16-20? Why?

Points which can be emphasised

Solving problems in the community demands quick and creative thinking. The process can be facilitated if we can discover some system.

34 Joining nine dots with four straight lines

Purpose

Many people are still steeped in strong traditions. As a result, in their approach to problem-solving they are still very much influenced by custom and habit. They are neither brave enough nor creative enough to break with habits which are unproductive. Through this game it is hoped:

Objectives

1 Participants will realise that in order to solve a problem it is often necessary to break away from existing customs and habits.

2 Participants realise that not all customs and habits are productive.

3 Participants realise that in solving a problem it must be considered from several angles.

Time

20-30 minutes

Place

Space for participants to write

Materials

Sheet of blank paper for each player
Pencil or ballpoint

The activity

Introduction

Give a brief account of the tendency for people to feel bound to habit, so that they lack the courage to attempt anything new.

● ● ●

● ● ●

● ● ●

Steps

1 Give a piece of blank paper to each participant.

2 Instruct each participant to make nine dots on their paper, as shown.

3 Instruct the participants to join these nine dots with four straight lines, without lifting their pencil.
4 After approximately ten minutes stop the exercise.

Discussion and conclusions

You can ask:

- Who failed to solve the problem? Why?
- Who was successful? Why?

Obviously if we limit ourselves to the limit set by the nine dots and do not attempt to go outside that 'limit', we cannot solve the problem.

Points which can be emphasised
In problem solving it is necessary to be creative and to have the courage to break with habit.

This idea can be pursued by extension in group discussion, in which participants examine existing social habits from the point of view of their advantages or disadvantages, and ideas or methods of breaking with those habits which are deemed disadvantageous.

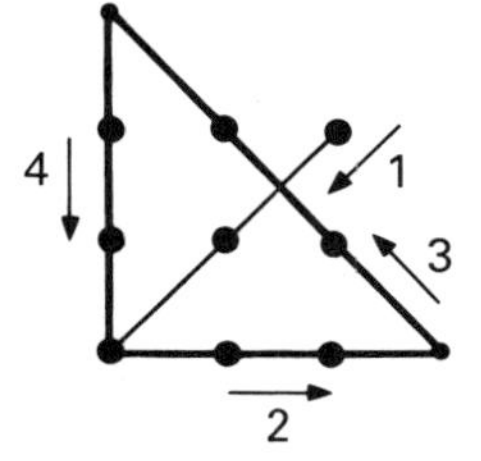

← *Key for trainer*

35 Connecting numbers

Purpose

So that skills and productivity can be increased, we must continuously learn by experience, and find the courage to innovate. An initial failure should not completely discourage us. We must always try again, learn again, until we are successful. Through this exercise it is hoped that:

Objectives

1 Participants will realise that to achieve a set aim requires perseverence, and constant hard work without losing heart.
2 Participants realise that each problem, because of its unique character, may require a different method of solution.

Time

30–40 minutes

Place

Room of sufficient size

Materials

Four forms for each participant. Three forms are the same: one form is different. Forms contain a different arrangement of numbers (see pages 86 and 87).
A large piece of paper and felt pen or blackboard and chalk

The activity

Introduction
Give instructions for playing.

① 53 39 15 28 16 40 54 6

27 51 5 2 26 52

13 17 3 41 38 14 50 30

37 29 25 18 4 42

49

7 23 31 55 46 36

35 43 57 22 12 34

11 19 45 8 44 24

47 33 20 32 58

21 9 59 60 56

48 10

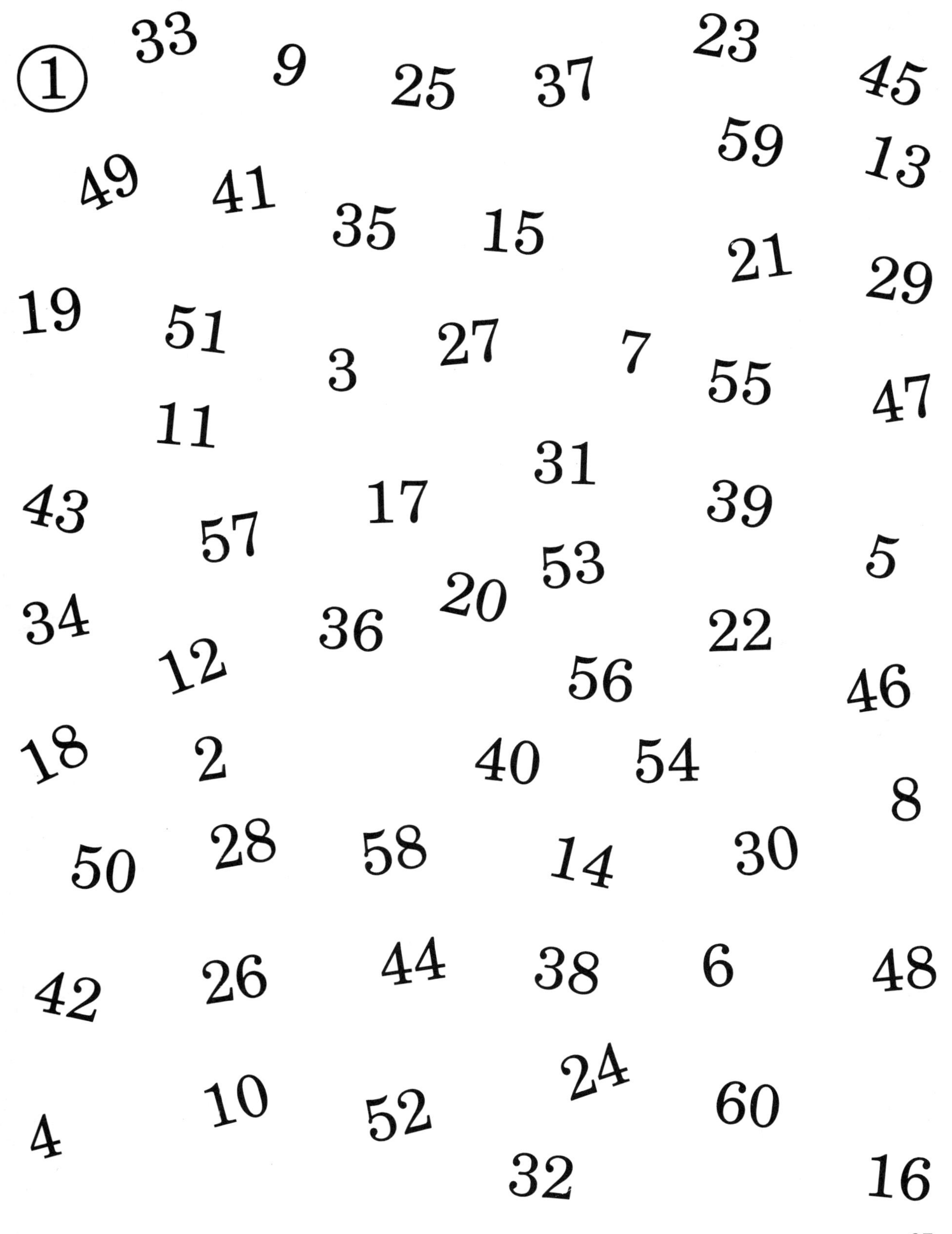
①
33
9
25
37
23
45
59
13
49
41
35
15
21
29
19
51
3
27
7
55
47
11
31
43
57
17
39
53
5
34
20
36
22
12
56
46
18
2
40
54
8
50
28
58
14
30
42
26
44
38
6
48
24
10
52
60
4
32
16

Steps

1 Distribute one of the following folded form 1's to each participant and tell them not to look at the form until you say begin.

2 Explain what each participant must do, that is draw a line joining the numbers in order of counting 1,2,3,4,5, etc. to the end.

3 Give the signal to begin.

4 After five minutes give the sign to stop work, and each participant notes his or her score by counting the numbers he or she is able to connect.

5 Distribute the same form and repeat the same process.

6 Distribute the same form again and repeat the same process.

7 Distribute the other form and repeat the same process.

Discussion and conclusions

Participants observe their own scores, i.e.

- Compare the results of the first with the results of the following two forms.

The score increases. Why?

- Compare the result of the third form with the fourth form.

The score decreases again. Why?

Points which can be emphasised

This exercise can be used to focus discussion on the idea that people will have a rising performance in a situation which is stable and without change, so that it becomes habitual because they have experience. But confronted with a new situation and new conditions, their performance declines. For this reason, perseverence and hard work is required in confronting problems arising from unfamiliar situations.

36 Making a hole

Purpose

A community worker must be creative so that activities will draw the interest of the community and other relevant parties. Thus it is hoped through this exercise that:

Objectives

1 Participants will realise that with perseverence and creativity something that looks impossible can be done.

2 Participants realise more fully the importance of working in detail and not just working out broad guidelines.

Time

45-60 minutes

Place

Any place

Materials

Half a piece of paper for each participant

The activity

Introduction

Explain creativity as an aspect of community participation.

Steps

1 Give each participant a piece of paper about 20 cm × 28 cm.

2 Tell the participants to make a hole in the paper, big enough for the paper in which the hole has been made to pass over the head and down to the feet.

3 The following conditions must be observed. Glue, or any other way of joining the paper, may not be used. When the person is in the hole, the paper must not break.

Discussion and conclusions

Points which can be emphasised

1 Something may appear impossible if we only think about it without trying to do it. If we persevere and try to do something, most things become possible.

2 We must always be creative.

3 The closer we tear the paper, the bigger the hole and the more easily our bodies will fit in, thus lessening the risk of the paper tearing. What does this tell us in relation to our programme? For example, if a programme is planned in detail and close attention is given to details when implementing the programme, the greater is our chance of success.

Key to the puzzle

1 Fold the paper exactly in the middle (lengthwise).

2 Tear the folded paper down the side, beginning at the folded edge or about one to one and a half centimetres from the edge of the open side. Be careful not to tear it right through to the opposite (open) side. Make the tear as close as possible to the edge of the paper.

3 Do the same thing again from the opposite side (the open side).

4 Open out the paper.

5 Tear each of the four pieces starting from the centre to the edge leaving again about one to one and a half centimetres at the edge. The tear must not extend to the sides.

Now you will have a piece of paper with a large hole in it made up of all the tears which you made.

NOTE: The trainer should try this first, before using it in training.

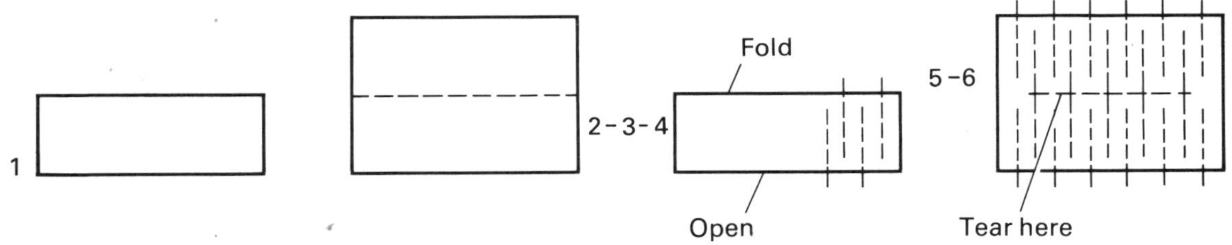

Often when we are asked to do something, we directly take on the task without really understanding what is required of us. This can have unfortunate results. By doing the 'Three Minute Test' it is hoped that:

Objectives

Participants will realise the importance of fully understanding a problem before working on it.

Time

20 minutes

Place

Any area sufficient for all the participants

Materials

One copy of the questions for each participant (Questions are on page 91)

The activity

Introduction

This test can be linked to the discussion on the implementation of programmes in the community - see Exercises 30, 31, 40, 41.

Steps

1 Distribute the 'Three Minute Test' face downwards to all the participants.

2 When everyone has a copy of the test, give the signal to begin.

3 Announce when three minutes are up and ask if any of the participants have finished.

4 You may extend the time allowed two or three times, or until two or three people have finished and realise they have been tricked.

Discussion and conclusions

Ask the participants what conclusion can be drawn from the test.

Points which can be emphasised
When we are asked to do something, we must try hard to understand fully what is required before we start work. Conversely, if we ask someone else to do something, we should check to see that they fully understand before they begin work. If participants are accustomed to taking tests, you can increase the pressure by announcing the end of the first minute and second minute.

Exercise from *Training and Continuing Education: A Handbook for Health Care Institutions,* and permission to use the exercise given by the Hospital Research and Educational Trust, 840 North Lake Shore Drive, Chicago, 111, USA.

Text: Three minute test

1 Read every question carefully before beginning.
2 Write your name on the top right hand corner of this page.
3 Draw a circle round the word 'name' in the sentence above.
4 Draw five small squares in the top left hand corner of this page.
5 Make a cross in each of the squares you have drawn.
6 Make a circle around each of the squares.
7 Place your signature below the heading on this piece of paper.
8 Write the word 'yes' at the end of the heading.
9 Put a circle round question number 7.
10 Make an X on the bottom left hand corner of this paper.
11 Make a triangle around the X that you have just made.
12 On the back of this paper calculate 70 × 32 =
13 Make a circle around the word 'paper' in the fourth question.
14 When you reach this sentence call your name out clearly.
15 If you consider you have followed directions properly, call out 'yes'.
16 On the back of this paper, calculate 107 plus 278 =
17 Put a circle round your answer.
18 Count aloud backwards from 10 to 1 in an ordinary voice.
19 Make three holes in this paper with the point of your pencil at the end of this sentence.
20 If you are obviously the first to reach this sentence call out in a clear voice 'I am a leader'.
21 Underline the even numbers on the left side of this paper.
22 After reading this sheet carefully, answer number 1 and number 2 only.

hanging foodstuffs

In the process of improving family health, people need certain knowledge related to daily living. This includes, among other things, knowledge of healthy practices, good agricultural procedures, methods of increasing nutrition for the family, etc. For the knowledge to be properly assimilated and thoroughly understood it can be explained by means of an exercise. Through this exercise it is hoped that:

Objectives

Participants will master certain knowledge concerning nutrition.

Time

20–30 minutes

Place

In the classroom or outside

Materials

A chair for all but one of the participants
Pictures of fruit, vegetables, and other foodstuffs (each picture approximately 15 × 15 cm). One picture for each participant
One pin for each participant

The activity

Introduction
After giving an explanation of nutritional food, ask participants to arrange their chairs in a circle. One chair is removed, so that there is one less chair than the number of participants.

Steps
1 Ask each participant to choose one picture and pin it on his chest.
2 Ask participants to sit.
3 The 'leader' stands in the centre of the circle and gives instructions to the participants.

4 Players with the fruit/vegetables that are referred to in the instructions must change chairs. The 'leader' must also try to get a chair. The player that fails to get a chair becomes the 'leader'.
5 The new leader stands in the centre of the circle and gives instructions to the others and so on.

Examples of instructions

- 'All fruits change places.'
- 'All vegetables that help to keep your eyes healthy change places.'
- 'All nutritious foods change places.'
- 'All foods that are body builders change places.'

Such instructions can be varied and graded according to the level of education of the participants and the content of the material which has been shared with them. They can, for example, be developed to increase mastery of knowledge in agriculture, health, etc.

Discussion and conclusions

The game can be concluded in the following ways:

- The trainer can review those aspects which were revealed during the game as not having been mastered properly.
- The trainer can ask each participant to provide a recipe using the food that he or she represents.

39 The square with the hole

Purpose

In order that participants begin to think about what they have learned, at the end of the session the participants are asked to set down a plan of action which they will put into practice in their own locality. In order to prepare for developing this plan of action, the following exercise is designed in the hope that:

Objectives

1 Participants will understand the dynamics of planning an activity which is to be implemented by someone else.
2 Participants will understand the dynamics of implementing work that has been planned by someone else.
3 Participants will understand the importance of communication in both giving and receiving instructions for the implementation of work following a plan.

Time

90 minutes

Place

One room for the Planning Team and one room for the Implementation Team

Frame of hollow square

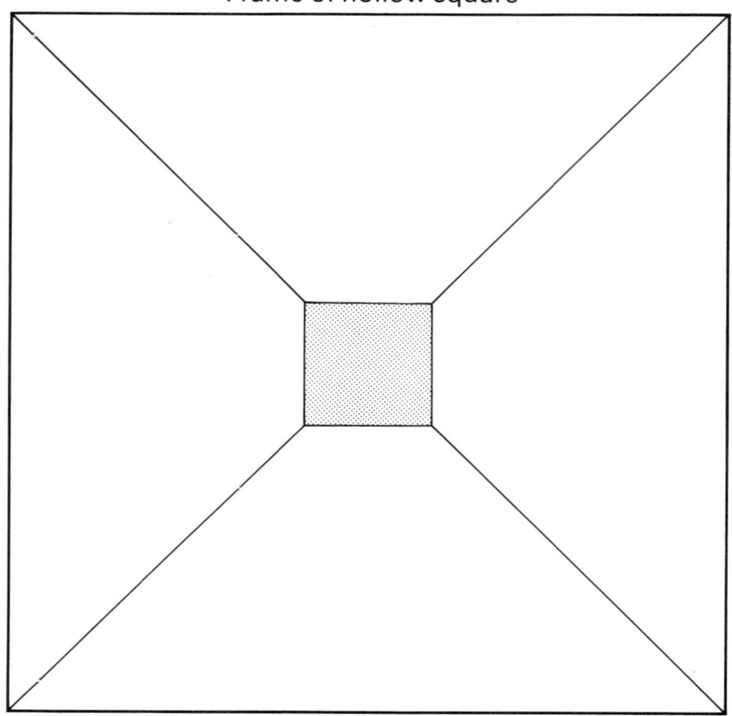

Key of hollow square

B D C C A A B D D B C A D A C B

Materials

1 A copy of the instructions for each member of the Planning Team (given on page 98).
2 A copy of the layout of the square for each member of the Planning Team (given on the page 94).
3 A copy of the key to the puzzle for each member of the Planning Team (given on page 94).
4 Four envelopes each containing four pieces of the square which are marked with the same letter of the alphabet. Each member of the Implementation Team is given one envelope.
5 A copy of instructions for the Implementation Team (given on page 100).
6 A copy of the instructions for each member of the Observation Team. Each member should also have a sheet of paper for notes.

The activity

Introduction
Briefly explain the difference between planning and implementing. Tell participants they are being asked to do an exercise related to planning. Participants are divided into three groups:

- planning group;
- implementing group;
- observing group (this group is divided into two, one group to observe the planning team and the other to observe the implementing team).

Steps
1 Choose four people to be the Planning Team and ask them to go to another room.
2 Choose four people to be the Implementation Team and ask them to wait in another room also. Give them the instructions for the Implementation Team.
3 Ask the remaining participants to form the Observation Team (a maximum of 15 people). This team should be divided into two groups. Group I are to observe the Planning Team, and Group II to observe the Implementation Team. Each participant is given a copy of the instructions for the Observation Team. Time should be allowed for them to read the instructions. Each member of the Observation Team might select one member of the Planning or Implementation Team to observe.
4 Explain to the Observation Team that they must stand or sit around the table used by the Planning Team and later the Implementation Team. The Observation Team is to observe and note down everything that happens for discussion when the exercise is completed.
5 The Planning Team is then called in, and asked to sit around the table. They are each provided with the sheet of instructions for the Planning Team, a copy of the final layout of the square, the key to the puzzle of the square, and one of the envelopes containing four pieces of the square.
6 Explain to the Planning Team that all the instructions are contained in the Instruction Sheet. Answer any questions pertaining to the

meaning of any sentence in the Instruction Sheet, but give no additional information.

7 Remind the Observation Team to remain silent, and not to offer assistance of any kind.

8 The process then begins to develop of its own accord. If there is more than one group, a competitive situation develops, and the trainer should note down the time taken by each group in order to compare their efficiency.

9 After the Implementation Team has completed the task or worked for the maximum time given, the trainer should initiate a discussion with the entire group. The Observation Team might be asked for their impressions, questions should be raised, and eventually both the Planning Team and the Implementation Team should be involved in the discussion. The trainer may, for example, ask:

- Was the Planning Team less efficient because it failed to do things that were not forbidden in the sheet of instructions? For example, it was not forbidden to make an illustration of the instructions on another sheet of paper.
- Did the Planning Team call the Implementation Team to share in the planning process? If there is more than one group, the reasons why one group won could also be discussed.

10 Give an analysis of the main points of the discussion, and points that were not touched on in the discussion.

Discussion and conclusions

Discussion

1 The trainer can ask the observers for their reports and the players for their thoughts about the game.

The following questions may help the players to express their thoughts:

a) How did the Implementors feel while they were waiting?

b) How did the Implementation Team feel when they failed to complete their task?

c) How did the Planning Team feel to see their plan not being carried out properly?

d) How did the Planning Team feel when the Implementors asked for assistance?

2 Based on the observations and the ideas of the participants, the trainer can discuss and reach a conclusion concerning those factors which are most important to the planning process.

Problems which may arise within the planning groups

1 General

The planning group might:

a) feel that their position is more important than that of the implementors, giving rise to unfortunate attitudes:

- belittling the efforts of the implementors;
- disinterest;

b) fail to consider, or ignore, the abilities or the feelings of the Implementors.

2 During planning

The planning group might:

a) fail to take sufficient account of time involved;

b) fail to take sufficient account of the expectations of the Implementors;

c) lack cooperation, spend too much time on giving precedence to personal opinions;

d) become too concerned with planning, so that orders do not get conveyed clearly;

e) or the reverse, become too busy giving orders, to the detriment of planning;

f) make the plan too general, and lacking in detail;

g) fail to consider probable sources of assistance, e.g. feel annoyed when asked questions by the Implementors (when in fact they should have been asked to help in the planning);

h) fail to share the work properly.

3 When giving instructions

The planning group might:

a) not be persuasive enough or be too dominating;

b) fail to give the Implementors sufficient opportunity to ask questions;

c) not use instructional aids effectively;

d) fail to provide a complete picture at the beginning, but move immediately into detail;

e) occasionally give instructions in such a way as to destroy cooperation among the Implementors.

4 During implementation

The planning group might:

a) fail to show any sense of shared responsibility for the implementation of the plan;

b) occasionally display annoyance towards the Implementors;

c) occasionally indicate:

- realisation of their own shortcomings;
- feelings of joint responsibility for errors;
- a desire to assist.

Problems which may arise within the implementation group

1 General

The implementing group might:

a) feel inferior to the Planners, causing unfortunate results because they are afraid to act.

2 While waiting for instructions

The implementing group might:

a) appear to have varied feelings, apprehension, stress, feeling of inadequacy etc.;

b) occasionally lack preparation for work sharing.

3 At the time of receiving instructions
The implementing group might:
a) lack confidence to ask questions;
b) have varied conceptions within the implementation group;
c) lack cooperation.
4 At the time of implementation
The group might:
a) forget what has been discussed concerning work sharing;
b) fail to work according to instructions;
c) be inclined to panic, causing confusion and making cooperation difficult.

The square with the hole

Instructions for the Planning Team
You have each received an envelope containing four parts of a puzzle. These, together with the pieces held by your colleagues, can be fitted together to make a square with a hole in the centre.

Your work
You have 20 minutes to:
1 plan how the 16 pieces that you have between you can be fitted together;
2 instruct the Implementation Team to carry out your plan. The Implementation Team can be called in at any time, but must not be called less than five minutes before they are told to start work.

General rules
1 The pieces of the puzzle must be in front of you all the time you are planning or giving instructions to the Implementation Team.
2 You may not touch or exchange pieces while planning or giving instructions.
3 You may not show the 'Key to the Puzzle' to the Implementation Team.
4 You may not arrange the pieces of the square because that is the work of the Implementation Team.
5 You must not mark the pieces in any way.
6 The members of the Implementation Team must also observe these rules.
7 Once you have told the Implementation Team to begin, you may not give additional directives or instructions. You may merely observe.

Instructions for the team observing the Planning Team

You will be observing a situation in which a Planning Team will decide how to solve a problem, and will instruct the Implementation Team to carry out their plan. The problem is how to arrange 16 puzzle pieces into one square with a hole in it. The Planning Team has the key to the puzzle, so that they know exactly how it can be done. However, the Planning Team may not do the puzzle, but must tell the Implementation Team how to do it.

You must observe only, without speaking.

Suggestions

1 You are expected to observe the general pattern of communication which occurs, and give special attention to one particular member of the Planning Team (while planning is underway) and one member of the Implementing Team (while they are working).

2 During planning, it will be useful to note:

a) Whether all members of the Planning Team actively participate?

b) What hinders the planning process?

c) How the Planning Team alot their time between planning and giving instructions to the Implementation Team? (When did they ask the Implementation Team to join them?)

3 During the time instructions are issued, it will be useful to note:

a) Which of the Planners gave the instructions to the Implementation Team? How was this decided upon?

b) How the Planners prepared and guided the Implementors for their task?

c) What parts of the plan were not communicated to the Implementation Team?

d) How effective were the orders given?

e) Did the Planners give the Implementors an opportunity to ask questions.

4 During implementation of the plan, it will be useful to note:

a) Were the instructions sufficiently clear?

b) What were the reactions of the Planning Team when they saw the Implementation Team carrying out their plan either accurately or incorrectly? (Remember that during this time the Planning Team may not speak.)

The square with the hole

Instructions for the Implementation Team

1 You are responsible for carrying out a duty set by a Planning Team of four members. The Planning Team will call you in to give you their instructions. If you wait for 20 minutes and have not yet been called, you may go in without waiting any longer. When you must start work, you may not receive any more instructions or ask any questions.

2 You must complete your task as quickly as possible.

3 While you are waiting to be called by the Planning Team, it might be useful for you to discuss with your colleagues (and make notes) concerning:

a) your feelings while waiting to be called, and while receiving instructions for work, the aim of which you do not know;

b) your ideas about how to make a compact and efficient team of your four members.

4 The notes you make now will probably be of use in subsequent discussion on the completion of the work.

The square with the hole

Instructions for the team observing the Implementation Team

You are to observe a situation in which a Planning Team will submit a plan that they have made. During observation you may not communicate in any way with the Implementation Team.

Suggestions

1 During the planning it will be useful to note:

a) What did the Implementation Team do while waiting to be called by the Planners?

b) What were the feelings between the members of the Implementation Team?

2 During the issuing of instructions it will be useful to note:

a) How did the Implementation Team react to the instructions?

b) Did any member of the Implementation Team ask a question?

3 During implementation of the plan it will be useful to note:

a) How did the members of the Implementation Team communicate with each other?

b) Did they cooperate well?

c) Did they conclude their work properly?

d) What were the reactions and attitudes within the team when they saw their work completed, either correctly or incorrectly?

40 Choosing a village for a community health programme

Purpose

Planning an actual programme calls on many of the skills which have been discussed in this book. This exercise with a health content and focus might be used near the end of the course in order that the participants can apply, practice and reinforce their learning experience.

Objectives

1 Participants will be encouraged to develop group decision-making activities.
2 Participants will become aware of the forces in a village which affect the success of a village worker programme.

Time

One hour or more depending on group size

Place

Classroom or similar large space for large group discussion and discussion areas for each small group to work

Materials

One copy of the Village Information Sheet for each participant
Blackboard and chalk or suitable substitutes such as large sheets of paper and felt pens

The activity

Steps
1 Introduce the exercise to the participants, and then divide the participants into small discussion groups and assign a location for each discussion group. Give each participant a copy of the Village Information Sheet.
2 Indicate that each group will have 20 minutes to select the village that they recommend for a Community Health Programme. They must support their recommendation with reasons for their choice.
3 After the groups have selected their village, reassemble the small groups into one large group. Have one member of each discussion group present their selection to the whole group. Record the selections and a summary of the reasons on the blackboard or on large sheets of paper.
4 Send the small groups back into their separate locations to reconsider their choices for ten minutes.
5 Reassemble the large group, check for changes in the village selection.

Discussion and conclusions

Points which can be emphasised
1 The response and openness of leaders, both formal and informal, is an important factor in choosing a village in which to begin a community based health programme.
2 It is important that at least some sections of the community show an interest in the possibility of change and development.
3 It is important to have a general understanding of the objectives of the community health programme when choosing which villages will be served.

The following questions might be asked in the discussion:

- What factors did each group use to make a decision?
- What are the most important factors we should consider in selecting the location of a programme?
- Can we make a list of these factors?
- Would the group like to gather more information to make a more definite choice? If so, what information?

4 The objectives of a Community Health Programme will determine which people will be served.

5 It is relevant to consider selecting a village which can possibly stimulate change in neighbouring villages in the future.

6 Communications and transportation facilities are important to help people get involved in development projects.

In conclusion, the various groups can be asked how they worked together to reach a decision. Also they may be asked if previous exercises helped in the development of the group's work and with relations among various group members.

Variations

1 Let some of the participants role play the members of each village. They can be 'visited' and 'interviewed' by the members of the groups making the village selection.

2 Let the groups establish the objectives for the Community Health Programme before introducing them to the four possible villages.

3 Provide the groups with a set of objectives and budget constraints before introducing the four villages.

Exercise adapted, with permission, from *A Manual of Learning Exercises for Use in Health Training Programmes in India*, by Dr. Ruth Harnar, A.C. Lynn Zelmer and Dr. Amy Zelmer. India: Voluntary Health Association of India, 1983.

Village information sheet (This sheet can be adapted to reflect the local situation)

You are members of a team to choose the location for a Community Health Programme. You will have a limited time to make your selection based on the information below.

Once you have selected the location for the Community Health Programme you must prepare a list of reasons for your choice. One member of your team will be asked to present your selection to the large group.

Village A
The Village Council is in favour of the programme. There is a traditional healer in the village. There is a religious leader in the village who is doubtful about the programme.

Village B
The leaders of the village are in favour of the programme. They have offered a location for the clinic. There is a traditional birth attendant in the village.

Village C
A teacher has invited the health team to the village. The leaders of the village feel that a meeting of the people has to be called to decide the issue, but they themselves are in favour of the programme.

Village D
The people are very traditional and against change. They are uncooperative with strangers and the government programme. Their health status is poor. The State Government is in favour of some programme being developed in this village by the team. An old lady living in the village is interested in the team's activities.

Map of the four villages

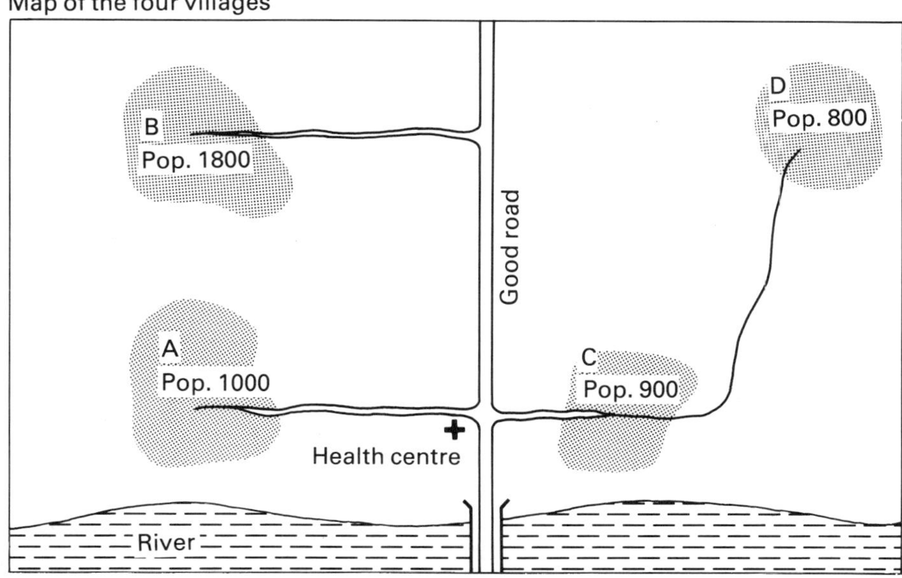

41 Assessing community needs

Purpose

This exercise is designed to help participants understand that the priority needs of the community are not always those which the planners have identified.

Objectives

1 The participants will recognise how their experiences and personal views affect their views about other people.
2 The participants will discover that often people with local life experiences (and perhaps less formal education) may have better insight into their own problems than the so-called expert outsider.

Time

60-90 minutes

Place

A place where participants can write individually

Materials

One copy of the following questionnaire for each participant

The activity

Introduction
This assessment is an example of planning in the community. Ask if any of the participants have done the exercise before. If so, ask the person to act as an observer.

Explain that participants are being asked to rank what they think people in a very poor slum area around a city see as their needs. When they have completed this task, the result of a real survey of the area will be given and they will be asked to compare their answers.

Steps
1 Pass out the questionnaire and ask everyone to answer it according to the instructions. Tell them to answer in the way in which they *imagine* the people in the slum area would answer the questions. (Repeat this last point.)

2 Tell the participants to mark their answers in the column on the left side. Give them about five minutes to complete this task.

3 Divide the participants into groups of five to seven and ask them to try to agree to a common ordering of priorities. Stress that the aim of this discussion is to reach an agreement in the group about the priorities. It is not merely to average individual answers. Tell participants they have about 20 minutes to do this.

4 Put up the list of correct answers given by the people in the slum area being studied (see below).

Answers from the people of the chosen area.

1 Food
2 Shelter
3 School fees
4 Clothing
5 Land
6 Money to expand their business
7 Clean water
8 Sanitation
9 Better standard of housing
10 Educational facilities

5 Ask participants to score their individual and group choices as follows: count how many points your answer is away from the correct rank given. That is your score. It makes no difference whether your score is above or below the correct answer. It is only the number of points in distance that counts. Then total your score. The *lower* your score, the more you understand the priorities of the people concerned.

Discussion and conclusions

You can base the discussion around the following questions:

- How did you feel about making judgement about a situation which was completely unfamiliar?
- Why did you agree to make those judgements?
- How relevant is it to apply an experience from one situation to another?
- Is it possible to make generalisations about poor people regardless of culture, location and history?

A final discussion may emphasise that experts and/or outsiders do not necessarily understand community needs better than the community itself. If we are going to make our plans relevant and useful, particularly to the very poor, we must find ways of learning from and with them.

Variation

This exercise can be shortened by only asking individuals, not groups, to do the ranking. In this case, the trainer should modify the questionnaire by deleting the Group Ranking column and the paragraph at the bottom of the questionnaire. The scoring procedure, the discussion and conclusion remain the same.

NOTE: This exercise can be adapted to local situations if the data is available.

Exercise adapted from *Training for Transformation, a Handbook for Community Workers*, by Anne Hope and Sally Timmel. Zimbabwe: Mambo Press, 1984.

Questionnaire

Priorities of the people in the slum area under study

The people were asked what problems they considered as the most important in their lives.

Instructions

Rank in order of what you think the *people in the valley* answered *as their first, second, third* priorities, etc. Place a number 1 by the one you think *they* ranked first, a number 2 by the one you think they ranked second, and so on, up to 10. Write your numbers in the left hand column.

	Individual Ranking		*Group Ranking*
A	______	Land	______
B	______	Clean water	______
C	______	Shelter	______
D	______	Clothing	______
E	______	School fees	______
F	______	Food	______
G	______	Money to expand business	______
H	______	Educational facilities	______
I	______	A better standard of housing	______
J	______	Sanitation	______

After the members of the group have finished working individually, form groups of five to seven people and try to arrive at a rank ordering *as a group*. The group has 20 minutes for this task.

Appendix 1 *Social preparation: Development of a community health programme*[1]

Mary P. Johnston

Major steps

A Promotion with the government
B Consolidation of the health staff
C Approach to the community
D Social preparation of the community
E Field preparation
a) Selection of initial programme
b) Collection of data about the community
c) Determination of problems to be tackled and setting priorities
d) Planning programme implementation
F Implementation of the programme
G Monitoring
H Assessment
I Revision
J Expansion of established programme
K Extension of programme to other communities
L Promotion and training in new area and repeat of whole process in new community

A Promotion with the government

- How can a doctor gain acceptance from peers and supervisors for ideas of experimentation with a community-oriented health programme?
- How can such a programme be integrated into the overall government programme?
- How can the doctor avoid friction with senior officials if the programme is eventually more successful than their programme?

→ *Government support must be gained in the initial stages of a programme.*

Purpose

1 To gain official support for the proposed programme.
2 To recruit government resources, including technical advice, facilities and funds.
3 To gain support from other disciplines at the same, or higher, levels in order to develop a comprehensive programme.
4 To integrate the programme into the government programme and prevent overlapping and competition.

Action

Discussion with senior government officials until some consensus is reached on concept of community health, and the idea to set up a community health programme in a specific locality is approved.

1 From S.B. Rifkin (editor), 'Health: the Human Factor', *Contact*, Special Series No. 3, June, 1980, published by the Christian Medical Commission, Geneva.

Information needed for successful action

1 Current government health policy, including opinions and statements from senior officials and international sources, on community health.

2 Overall plan of implementation should include ideas on:

- organisation/framework within which programme will be developed;
- financial aspects;
- advantages over current system, e.g. wider coverage, more economical use of staff, cheaper. (In discussing advantages, factors of special interest and importance to the government officials should be emphasised.)

3 Criteria for the selection of locality for trial should include the following:

- the community to be served should be manageable, viable and, preferably, an established administrative unit such as a village;
- the unit should have economic potential;
- it should have strong, active, honest leadership;
- it should be strategically placed to enable expansion to other areas.

B Consolidation of health staff

- How will staff who have worked for years in a curative service accept a programme with a new orientation?
- How can a doctor secure the support of the rest of the health team for a new programme? No doctor can implement a community health programme alone.

→ *It is important to consolidate the staff of the health service.*

Purpose

1 To prepare the health staff for a programme oriented to the community.

2 To provide the staff with skills required for community work.

3 To form a cohesive team.

Action

Retaining the staff of the health service, including, if necessary, its reorganisation.

Information needed for successful action

1 On forming an effective team

A team which understands and accepts the new approach and feels confident in implementing it is needed. The team may consist of:

- a doctor, or other team leader;
- paramedics, and nursing staff;
- social worker; and
- agriculturalist (or other technical worker, depending on local community needs).

If it is not possible to increase staff, current staff can perhaps be equipped with extra skills.

2 On training content and methods

a) Training should achieve changes in attitudes, through:

- statements proving government interest in, and support of, new orientation;
- proof of need for new orientation, e.g. clinic statistics indicating limitations of existing service, reasons for non-attendance at health service etc.;
- contact with community health workers;
- visits to successful community health programmes.

b) Training should provide skills in:

- approaching the community;
- communicating with the community;
- working together with the community;
- planning;

- maintaining and developing a programme; and
- simple administrative skills.

c) Training methods could include:

- discussions;
- exposure to situations followed by reflection on the situation;
- problem solving; and
- role playing, etc.

C Approach to community

- How can a health programme become a community based programme?
- How can a doctor help the community to tackle its own health problems?

→ *It is important that the community be approached in the very early stages of development of the programme. Close cooperation between the health service and the community is essential.*

Purpose

To gain the support and the direct, active participation of the community in developing the programme.

Action

Health worker approaches the community leadership, if possible both formal and informal. [**or**]

Health worker is approached by the community leader. (This is only likely to happen in a community where a successful programme has already been established in the vicinity.)

Information needed for successful action

1 For the identification of a sympathetic community leader, criteria should include:

- interest in health;
- active interest in community welfare;
- innovative ideas; and
- influence in community.

2 Method of approach

Discussions should focus on:

- particular issues, events occurring in community (deaths, epidemic, special day);
- statistics from local clinic (high disease incidence, disease patterns); and
- examples of programmes in other areas.

Important factors

1 Official approval of local leader is prerequisite.

If a direct approach to formal leaders is not possible, or unsuccessful, informal leaders, e.g. teachers, religious leaders, may be approached. When they are convinced about the new ideas, they can be encouraged to influence the formal leadership.

A government superior (e.g. a district head) may be the needed contact person in other cases.

2 It is unusual for the initiative in setting up a health programme to be taken by the community. But where this occurs and the existing health workers are unresponsive to approaches from village leader, the help of a more senior official, e.g. senior doctor, senior government official, could be requested to convince the health worker, through discussions and visits to successful programmes.

D Social preparation of the community

- How can the whole community (as opposed to leaders only) participate in programme development?

- How can a health worker make contact with members of the community? What channels can be used?
- How can the health worker avoid the danger of arousing a feeling within the community that their cooperation is desired merely to further the ambitions of the health worker?

→ *Social preparation of the community is crucial to the success of a programme.*

Purpose

1 To develop community understanding of the basic aims of the programme.
2 To encourage the community to reach a decision to implement a programme based on its particular needs.
3 To mobilise local resources.

Action

1 Informal individual and group discussions about community problems and needs and the proposed community health programme, held between health worker and leaders in the community.
2 Community leaders, assisted by the health worker, then introduce the idea of the community health programme, informally and through community groups and meetings, to community members.
3 Discussions should be held until a decision is reached by community leaders and community members (if possible) to implement the community health programme.

Information needed for successful action

1 Influential community leaders include:
- formal leaders, e.g. government, traditional, religious; and
- informal leaders, e.g. religious, educated, wealthy, political.

The support of both formal and informal leaders is important.

2 Existing 'effective' community organisations have:
- ongoing activities;
- membership representing the whole community;
- sound leadership; and
- a flexible programme.

Approaches should be made to such organisations as the community health programme could possibly be inserted as the programme of one of these organisations.

3 Efforts to identify community problems and needs may include investigations on:

Health:
- general observation, especially of deficiencies, including malnutrition, particularly in the under-fives' group;
- noting major illnesses as recalled by members of the community (and indicative of the high incidence of certain diseases);
- collecting data on number and causes of deaths and incidence of epidemics (or threat of);

Education:
- asking local teachers about their problems;
- comparing number of school-age children with number of school attenders;
- checking drop-out figures and reasons;

Transport/Communication:
- checking distance from nearest market, school and other important facilities;
- checking means of contact with, and transport to, secondary health care facilities;

Agriculture:

- comparing yields with expected average yields of area;
- asking farmers for their opinions of problems and needs;
- observing general conditions in the field.

4 Customary ways in which the community solves problems
When obtaining information about major needs and concerns, also ask about ways in which the community has tried to meet these needs. Possibly the customary ways of solving problems can be developed and incorporated into the new programme. E.g. If a community collects funds to cover funeral expenses, this could be developed into a simple insurance scheme in which subscriptions are collected to provide health care for the living.

5 Methods by which the community reaches decisions.

a) Determine which groups/group leaders are most influential in the community as they are the best channels through which to gain community support.

b) Determine which is the officially recognised decision-making body/committee through which the final decision for acceptance of the programme should be made.

c) Determine the type and frequency of group meetings. If the decision is reached in a formal meeting attended by a large proportion of leaders and community members, it will have stronger backing and support.

d) Determine whether decision-making is:

- a decision by the recognised leader;
- majority vote; or
- discussion culminating in unanimous decision. Whichever decision-making method is used, it is important that as many community members and leaders as possible understand and agree with programme.

Important factors

1 The health worker must have an open, friendly attitude, indicating willingness to learn about the community from the people.

2 The introduction of the proposed programme should always be through discussions on major concerns of the community. Through discussions, assess what these are and start there. E.g. A volunteer health promoter programme could be suggested as an answer to the problem of long distances from the health service.

3 In a community where health is not a major priority, e.g. a poor, isolated community, implementation of a health programme may have to be postponed until other more pressing needs felt by the community are met. E.g. An agricultural programme which raises crop yields may provide the community with the economic means enabling them to use the proposed health service.

Non-formal education may increase awareness and understanding of the advantages of healthier living.

NOTE: At this stage, the community health programme is accepted in principle only. Details of the programme have not yet been worked out.

E Field preparation

→ *Joint preparation of the field, including selection of a limited area for trial, collection of data, determination of priorities, and planning is important.*

E.1 Selection of initial programme area

- How can a community be convinced that a programme is feasible and of benefit to them?

- How can ideas be tried out without their failure jeopardising the whole programme?
- How can programme implementors gain confidence from experience?

Purpose

To select a restricted area, with high probability of success, for trial.

Action

Community leaders and health worker reach a decision on locality for trial programme.

Information needed for successful action

1 Nature of appropriate locality

The site most conducive to successful implementation would be:

- an existing community, preferably a small administrative unit, e.g. subhamlet or village;
- manageable in size;
- an economically viable community; and
- one with good leadership.

(In subsequent development of the programme in other areas, weaknesses can be overcome by many means, e.g. an economically weak unit could be combined with a vigorous and thriving village.)

2 Nature of local leadership

The leadership of the trial unit should be:

- authoritative;
- honest;
- actively interested in the welfare of the community; and
- supported by the community.

(In subsequent development of the programme, weak leadership can be overcome by many means, e.g. by working through strong informal leaders with formal leader as figurehead.)

E.2 Collection of data about the community

- How can the community and health worker learn more about local conditions?
- How can a programme be based on real and felt needs of a community?

→ *It is important to collect relevant data about the community together with members of the community.*

Purpose

1 To provide baseline data.

2 To enable local leaders to become more aware of conditions in their community.

3 To increase the awareness of the community of problems facing them.

Action

1 Prepare simple questionnaire suited to local needs and adapted to the skills of the interviewers.

2 Inform leaders of the purpose of the questionnaire and reason for collecting data.

3 Selection of interviewers, preferably from the community.

4 Training of interviewers.

5 Data collection.

6 Tabulation and analyses of data.

Information needed for successful action

1 Community to be covered

It is important to collect data from the whole community if conditions are favourable. However, if community to be covered is too large, sampling methods should be used. These methods can be studied in a handbook on surveys.

2 Content of survey

The data should cover both the community in general and individual families. On community, items such as number of families, average family size, public facilities and vital statistics, should be covered. On families, information on factors such as number in family, ages, education, occupations, income conditions, health status, environment, mother and child care, agriculture and social customs could be included.

3 Method of composing questionnaire

- Questionnaire should be short and seek only information which can be used either directly for programme planning, or as an indicator of success for the monitoring of the programme.
- Ensure that the questions have one meaning only and will bring the answers required.
- Ensure that questions are not suggestive of a particular answer.
- Ensure that answers are given in a way which is easily tabulated, e.g. by using simple indicators, such as + = good; ± = fair; – = bad.

4 Selection of interviewers

If possible, community members should do the interviewing. Choose community members with:

- ability to approach fellow community members,
- ability to ask questions honestly and record answers accurately, and
- interest in programme and time to spare.

If volunteer health workers have been formed before collection of data, this task should be given to them to increase their awareness of community conditions, and to provide a basis for them to plan their programme.

5 Content and method of training interviews

Training should include:

a) reasons for asking questions in questionnaire;

b) guidance on how to explain need for data collection to community members;

c) guidelines for interviewing techniques, including information on how to:

- create an open, friendly atmosphere,
- ask open and closed questions,
- prevent bias in answers,
- cross-check answers; and

d) instruction on how to fill in questionnaire.

Training methods could include: discussion, role play, trial run followed by discussion of problems.

6 Method of collecting data

a) Coverage: The capacity of one interviewer in a rural area where homes are widely separated is, at a rough estimate, 10 families a week;

b) Timing: Home visits should be geared to times when community members are at home;

c) Supervision: Supervision of interviewers is important to maintain their enthusiasm and increase validity of data. Such supervision should include spot checks of difficult questions, close recording of time taken in interview, number of interviews conducted, etc. Each interviewer should keep his or her own records. Daily discussion of results is helpful for increasing skills.

7 Method of tabulation

Tabulation can be done by community members with guidance from health workers. Response frequency for each question should be counted and tabulated.

Respondents can be divided into groups based on employment, size of family, education of parents, or other relevant factors.

8 Method of analysis

Each item in the tabulation can be evaluated according to simple criteria, such as: good/bad, sufficient/insufficient, satisfactory/unsatisfactory. Those items assessed as bad, insufficient and unsatisfactory are raw material on which to base plans for programme.

Important factors

1 Data collection is important, but if problems arise (e.g. suspicious community leader, suspicious community members, inappropriate timing), data can be collected in stages as the need arises for specific programmes (e.g. under-fives' programme, environmental improvement programmes).

2 Data collection could also be postponed until volunteer health promoters have been trained. Advantages of using volunteer health promoters:

- they are known by the community;
- they have an intimate knowledge of the community;
- they can gain increased awareness of problems; and
- they can obtain data for planning their programmes.

NOTE: It is especially important to safeguard bias if health promoters or other local people are used.

E.3 Determination of problems to be tackled and setting priorities

- How can a community set priorities in the face of a large number of problems?
- How does one select the 'right' initial activity?

→ *It is important to begin a programme with a relevant activity important to a significant number of people.*

Purpose

1 To initiate a dynamic programme.

2 To select a small-scale, low-cost activity which will produce quick results.

3 To provide stimulation for continuing development of the programme.

Action

1 Presentation of survey results to community leaders and community members (if possible).

2 Determination of priorities and initial activity.

Information needed for successful action

1 Reporting survey results

Survey results should be reported back to the community in a form understandable to them. A descriptive, non-technical form highlighting problems and also potentials may be most effective. If possible, the report should be made both orally and in writing. The oral presentation to community leaders, both formal and informal, provides a good opportunity for discussion of major community problems, both those in the report and those felt by the community.

2 Criteria for determining priorities to be considered

Four simple criteria can be considered:

- What is the incidence of the problem in the community?
- How serious is it as a health problem? (Opinion of health worker)
- What importance does the community place on the problem?
- How difficult is it to overcome? (Management considerations)

The health worker together with the community can make a simple analysis of results by evaluating each problem according to the above criteria using a scale of 0–3. The scores are then multiplied to gain a final score. Priorities are determined, the problem with the highest score gaining first priority.

As far as possible, the key members of the community should be involved in determining priorities. Their involvement in all decision making will increase the validity of the decisions and increase their commitment to the programme. Both short- and long-term priorities should be determined to provide the vision of a continually developing, comprehensive programme.

3 Criteria for selecting initial activity:

- low cost;
- limited to small, feasible size;
- ability to produce results within ± six months.

Using these criteria, plans should be realistic and within the scope of the community. Hence success will be maximised, resulting in a relationship of trust and confidence between the community and the health worker.

It is important also that the initial activity should stimulate further activities, leading to a more comprehensive programme, e.g. that a nutrition programme might stimulate improvements in agricultural techniques, or a savings programme stimulate small productive activities.

E.4 Planning programme implementation

- As experience is an invaluable teacher, how can members of the community acquire skills in planning and management though experience?

→ *It is important to make clear and feasible plans with community members.*

Purpose

1 To make plans acceptable to both the community and health service.

2 To involve all parties in planning and implementation.

3 To increase community skills.

Action

1 Meeting of community leaders, community members (if possible) and health worker to make plans for implementation, or invitation of community leaders.

2 Setting up committee and administration, including a division of responsibilities.

Information needed for successful action

1 Existing organisations in the community

If possible, the programme should be set up through existing organisations.

If necessary, these could be reactivated, given new functions, etc.

Only when this proves impossible should a new organisation be created to carry out the programme.

2 Type of framework for programme

Examples of possible frameworks within which to set up a programme are as follows:

a) A simple health insurance scheme can provide a framework for developing a comprehensive community health programme, e.g. environmental improvements, credit union, volunteer health promoters, under-fives' weighing, etc., can all be built into the framework as community awareness increases and needs arise.

b) A volunteer health promoters' programme could also provide the framework for similar activities, as well as improved use of home gardens, under-fives' nutrition programme, health posts, etc.

F Implementation of the programme

• How can the community best be made aware of its own strengths and resources, and encouraged to use those resources?

→ *To build the community's conviction of ownership and responsibility it is important to mobilise maximum community resources.*

Purpose

1 To carry out plans efficiently with active support and participation of the community.

2 To mobilise local potential and resources.

3 To develop management and other skills in the community.

Action

Community leaders, committee and health worker meet to discuss the implementation of plans, including steps, timetable, division of tasks, manpower use etc. (This may take several meetings.)

Information needed for successful action

1 Simple methods of planning and management.

2 Methods of conducting a meeting so that those present contribute and plans stem from joint discussion.

Preferably, these meetings should be called and led by the committee. If there is a division of responsibilities amongst the members, all will have a meaningful contribution to make to the meeting.

3 Resources available within the community and those from without the community (if required).

These include: materials, equipment, funds, skills, technical knowledge and manpower.

Data collected in initial stages should provide details on resources within the community.

Important factors

1 Plans should only be carried out *after* the community is prepared, i.e. after social preparation and field preparation are completed.

2 The community leaders and members should be responsible for making the plans, not the health worker.

3 The role of the health worker is:

• to assist the committee in considering problems which may arise during implementation;

• to provide technical information; and

• to 'prod' the committee (if needed), e.g. if committee chairman 'forgets' to call a meeting.

G Monitoring

• What should be done if action planned together is not implemented?

• How can the community closely follow the progress of a programme?

→ *Ongoing monitoring of the progress of activities is important.*

Purpose

1 To follow the progress of implementation of plans.

2 To study the relationship between input, output and impact.

3 To stimulate the community through continual feedback.

4 To revise methods, if necessary.

Action

1 During implementation of the programme, progress is monitored by trained community members.

2 The community, community leaders and health worker meet periodically to discuss the results of the monitoring.

Information needed for successful action

1 Simple methods of monitoring

It is essential to work out a simple recording system which is meaningful to the community, and can be kept by community members. Community members should be trained in the use of the system.

2 Effective ways to provide feedback of information.

The opportunity must be provided for the community to receive regular reports of progress, e.g. at community meetings, at regular committee meetings, through poster displays.

Informal contacts with community leaders should also be used for feedback of information about the programme. Both formal and informal contacts provide an opportunity for the community to give feedback to the committee on reasons for success or failure to progress.

H Assessment

- What steps should be taken if a programme becomes static because the community loses interest and no new ideas arise?
- How can the community assess the results of its programme?

→ *Assessment of end results of activities is important for programme development.*

Purpose

1 To assess whether results of activities within the programme are satisfactory and meeting the aims of the programme.

2 To stimulate the development of other activities.

Action

1 Community leaders, committee and health workers meet for discussion of results of activity. (In long-term programme, these meetings are held periodically.)

2 Community meetings are held by community leaders where results of assessment by committee are discussed, and ideas on expansion of the programme based on results of assessment are developed.

Information needed for successful action

1 Simple method of assessment

Criteria for measuring progress could include:

- change of disease pattern;
- infant mortality rate;
- incidence of illness in community;
- improvements in environment;
- increased community participation in health programme;
- community's use of service (accessibility and acceptability); and
- effectiveness of service (cost and benefit).

Data on results achieved through programme is compared with baseline data collected in initial stage of programme.

Important factors

The assessment must help the community to understand the results of their programme.

Therefore:

1 Community leaders (and if possible community members) should be involved in making the assessment. (E.g. the monitoring records could be used.)

2 The assessment must be prepared and presented in a form understood by the community.

3 The assessment must be reported back to the community members.

I Revision

NOTE: This step is only necessary if assessment reveals that an activity is not meeting programme objectives, or programme objectives are not meeting community needs.

→ *It is important to maintain a dynamic programme which meets the changing needs of the community.*

Purpose

1 To increase the effectiveness and efficiency of the programme.

2 To reorganise the programme to meet the needs of the community more closely.

Action

In a meeting of the community leaders, committee and health worker, decisions are made on the need for revision and methods of revision.

Information needed for successful action

1 Aspects needing revision.

These will be evident from the results of the monitoring and assessment.

2 Alternative activities which are more appropriate.

Important factors

A community is never static; community needs are continually changing. Therefore a flexible programme is required, and programme implementors must be openly willing to change and revise programme as needed. A programme should be dynamic, never static.

J Expansion of established programme

- How can the causes of problems be attacked? For example, the community not only collects blood samples to detect malaria infection, but also works towards the eradication of mosquitoes.
- How can the community reach the goal of healthier living?

→ *It is important to tackle root causes of problems through developing a comprehensive programme.*

Purpose

1 To improve the quality of the programme, through expanding the number and type of activities.

2 To meet health needs of the community more adequately through a comprehensive programme.

Action

In periodic meetings, possibly at the same time as assessment, community leaders, committee and health worker, propose, select and plan further activities. (This meeting is preferably called by community leaders.)

Information needed for successful action

1 Methods of motivating community leaders and members to propose new activities may include:

- visits to more advanced programmes;
- development of a new activity in a limited locality, followed by encouragement of satisfied community members to stimulate other localities to follow their example; and
- competitions.

2 Ways of encouraging community members to take more initiative should be based on increasing their awareness about the community they live in and its problems.

This can be achieved by:

a) training selected community members as volunteer health promoters so that they will have a deeper and more critical understanding of the causes of health problems and ways to overcome them;

b) using important events to stimulate action, e.g. Independence Day preparations could include work on environmental improvements; and

c) using dramatic events, e.g. an outbreak of an epidemic or a death, to increase awareness and stimulate action to prevent a further occurrence of the same problem.

Important factors

Before implementing any new activity, it is essential to repeat the steps of social preparation and field preparation.

K Extension of programme to other communities

- How can other communities benefit from the experience gained earlier by an established community health programme?
- Who is responsible for the development of a community health programme in other communities?
- Who can find time to work with other communities, given the limited resources available?

→ *Successful activities should be extended to cover a wider population.*

Purpose

To motivate leaders in other communities to adopt a community health programme.

Action

Exposure of key people from other communities to the original programme.

Information needed for successful action

1 Media for promoting contact with other communities could include:

a) Observation visits to original programme.

b) Contact between leaders of a community which has not yet begun a programme with experienced leaders of the community health programme.

c) Government channels, e.g. introduction of programme at meeting of formal leaders.

d) Mass media.

e) Audio-visual aids, e.g. filmstrip describing community health programmes.

f) Public meetings, e.g. seminars, workshops.

g) Printed brochures, manuals and other materials.

2 Early interest and motivation can be reinforced by the following:

- government instruction which provides backing for the programme. To avoid negative effects of instruction from above, the community should be prepared to receive it;
- provision of more detailed oral and written information, e.g. full description of how to implement programme.

Important factors

1 This step may be carried out only when the initial programme is firmly established, i.e. when:

- the community feels they are profiting from the programme;
- community leaders and members are able to relate their experiences; and
- intensive supervision is no longer required.

2 It is preferable that communities take the initiative in beginning the process of developing a programme in their area.

L Promotion and training in new area, followed by repeat of whole process

• How can limited resources best be used to equip others to develop a satisfactory programme?

• How can the initiators of a new programme learn from the successes and failures?

→ *A newly developing programme can benefit from the experience gained through an existing programme.*

Purpose

1 To establish the programme in the new area on a firm foundation.

2 To provide a basic understanding of the philosophy and broad content of the programme.

3 To share information on setting up the programme in a new area.

4 To encourage the development of a flexible, dynamic programme related to local conditions and needs in the new area.

Action

1 Community leaders and/or health workers in new area commence promotion with the government and approaches to the community.

2 Training of key people from new area, including community leaders and health workers.

Information needed for successful action

1 On identity and characteristics of key formal and informal leaders.

2 Appropriate training methods and content.

Trainers should be people with experience in existing programme, including health workers, community leaders, volunteer health promoters. The curriculum and organisation of the training should be determined by trainers and trainees together, based on needs of trainees. Training material should include basic philosophy and broad outline of programme only, as it is important that the details of the programme should be determined by the local community, according to local conditions.

Important factors

1 It is important to be aware of the disadvantages which could arise from using a programme as a training field, and attempt to forestall them. Possible disadvantages could be: oversaturation of the field; jealousy from other areas which are not used for training; or development of excessive pride and self-satisfaction resulting in an inability to receive any new ideas from outside.

2 The training is followed by social preparation, field preparation and all the subsequent steps outlined above.

3 Continuous contact between those involved in the existing programme with those developing the new programme is valuable to both parties.